Retail Selling
Ain't Brain Surgery,
It's Twice As Hard

Nine steps to successful sales relationships

by James E. Dion
Dionco Inc.

Published by
Dionco Inc.
300 West Grand Avenue
Suite 408
Chicago, Illinois 60610
http://www.dionco.com

Production Coordinator: Cathy Ramsamujh
Design by: Surge Ramsamujh
Edited by: Megan Williams

ISBN 0-9711013-0-2

Printed in the United States of America

Acknowledgements

This book would not have been written without the help and understanding of many people in my life. I would like to thank Richard Boron and Paul Barnett who, almost forty years ago, taught me the real basics of retail selling. Megan Williams for her gentle editing, Surge Ramsamujh for his taste and skill in design, Cathy Ramsamujh for all her work on the original and every version that followed! And thanks to my two incredible children, Julie and Jamie who have always inspired me, and last but not least, Stefania, my wife who has enriched my work and made my life complete.

Contents

Preface

In many ways I have been writing this book for almost twenty-five years. My career in selling began in 1964 at a small store on the south side of Chicago. I certainly was not committed to selling at the time. As a matter of record, I was probably one of the worst clerks ever to grace the sales floor. I got into retail for the same reason many young people do: It was an easy job to get, and you did not get dirty. I guess I viewed it as an effortless way to make some (very little) money to pay tuition bills.

I stayed with that store throughout university and even into my first teaching job. It was not until I started working in a hotel, during graduate school, that I began to understand the role of selling and service in my life. It took the experience of landing in a Sears store in Richmond Hill, Ontario, and starting my first day of selling in the Men's Wear Department, with nine years of University behind me, to realize that I was where I really wanted to be.

You see, being trained as a psychologist, I thought that helping people meant helping through therapy. What I had learned in retail, however, was that helping people could also consist of making small, but very real differences in their lives by ensuring that what they spent their money on would make them happier. This may seem lofty or even sugar-coated, but I assure you, a Professional Sales Associate can make as much difference in peoples lives as any doctor, lawyer or, indeed, therapist. The Professional Sales Associate sees thousands of people each year, and if even half of these encounters bring joy or fulfillment, however small, to another person, then the profession of selling has earned its place among the helping professions.

I first discovered the following passage about 12 years ago, although it was written over 130 years ago. It says a lot about the business of being a merchant and to me, it says a lot about the impact a Professional Sales Associate can have on society. It was written by J. Hamilton Fyfe in 1864.

The Caravan and The Fleet

"The good merchant," says quaint old Thomas Fuller, "is one who by his trading claspeth the Islands to the Continent, and one country to another; an excellent gardener, who makes England bear wine, and oil, and spices; yea herein he goes beyond nature in causing that omnis fert omnia tellus[1]." The mission of the merchant is indeed, when rightly viewed, one of the most important of the occupations of [wo]men, and has in all ages exerted a deep influence on the progress of society and the destiny of nations. Geologists have begun to discover that the steady flow of water is, after all, accountable for greater terrestrial changes than spasmodic bursts of volcanic fire. Thus, too, Commerce, in its earnest, ceaseless, silent, undemonstrative way, has produced more momentous and permanent revolutions among the peoples of the earth than war, dazzling us by the visible signs of its victories and desolations.

It was Commerce which quickened the primitive faculties of [wo]man, and brought the early races into communion with each other; which opened up the rich and varied treasury of India to peoples further from the rising sun; which made princes of the camel-drivers of Babylon and the fishermen of Tyre; which raised up imperial cities on the hot sands of the African sea-shore, on the muddy refuse of the Po, and on the quaking marshes of Holland; which made London the capital

---

[1] Each of us carry all earthly things.

of an empire extending to the furthermost ends of the earth; which first developed and then checked the rapid growth of the giant Republic of the New World. Agriculture, manufacture, navigation, most of the arts and many of the sciences, owe their origin to the promptings of Commerce, and their progress to its stimulus. Alternately the nations have taught and learned; and along with material products, religion, poetry, and philosophy have been disseminated by means of the caravan and the fleet.

There does not, at first sight, appear to be much heroism and romance in the occupation of a merchant; but it is not difficult, on reflection, to discover that there may be, and often is, both; and it is well that [s]he should not lose sight of the great influences [s]he may be setting at work, and the responsibility [s]he is incurring, even when engaged in seemingly commonplace and trivial details of routine work.[2]

(Emphasis mine.)

• • •

There are no schools that can teach you to be a Professional Retail Sales Associate. Most Professional Sales Associates have acquired their skills on the job and by attending company training classes. There are not a lot of books or training seminars available to Sales Associates, so this book was written to give you the skills you need to build a profitable and successful career as a Retail Sales Associate.

While this book contains all you will need to build a solid base of selling skills, the ingredients you must provide are your commitment and product knowledge.

---

[2] J. Hamilton Fyfe, Merchant Enterprise, or The History of Commerce from the Earliest Times. London: 1864.

Commitment will require not only reading the book, but also trying out the practice sections by yourself and with fellow Sales Associates. Commitment is also about self motivation, keeping yourself up and interested in the store and the Customer. Most Professional Sales Associates are driven by an internal engine that sets new and challenging goals each day. If you truly want to be successful in selling, you will set these personal goals and do your best every day to exceed them.

Product knowledge, as you will soon learn, is one of the most difficult and important parts of selling, and you will have to spend considerable time acquiring it. Learning to sell is deceptively simple: Once you learn the nine steps described in the book, it appears to be a very easy process. But retail selling is really more complex than brain surgery. As a brain surgeon, once you have seen one brain, you have seen most all brains. There is not much difference between humans in physiology. While there is a lot to learn as a brain surgeon, and you must have steady hands, once you have learned the brain physiology, it rarely changes.

But retail selling is really more complex than brain surgery.

I make this point not to trivialize brain surgery, as it is a very complex and honorable profession. But as a Professional Retail Sales Associate, you should realize that your profession is also honorable and extremely complex and often twice as hard, as you are faced with a completely different personality and set of challenges with each Customer you meet.

The purpose of this book is to give you the tools to become a Professional Retail Sales Associate. I do think that there are heroism and romance in retail selling, and that you can affect many lives for the better when you know how to satisfy Customers' needs. However, I can only give you the tools, you have to take them, use them and build your Professional Career. Good Luck.

... you can affect many lives for the better when you know how to satisfy Customers' needs.

You should also note that this book is meant to be read and practiced one chapter at a time. Read a chapter every few days and work on the practice section. In a few weeks you will be on your way to happier Customers and more personal satisfaction!

Introduction to Retail Selling

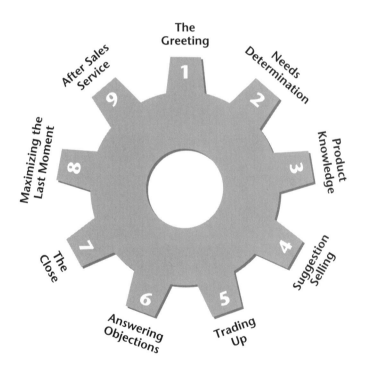

> The best augury of a man's success
> in his profession is that he thinks it the
> finest in the world.
>
> *George Eliot, English novelist*

Selling is a profession

Selling in a retail store has not been recognized as a real profession. Yet it is a profession to millions (over five million people in North America), and as far as I am concerned, it is one of the most rewarding professions there is. The words Sales Associate imply two things: First, and foremost, the job is about selling and second, the job is about a partnership and sharing with others in the store.

There are not too many jobs that provide a person with a pleasant work environment and the opportunity to make hundreds of people happy every day. While it is true that many stores have not yet realized how important the Sales Associate is to their business, more and more are discovering that a well-educated Sales Associate is critical for success in the retail industry today. Each and every sale that is made contributes to the success of the store's business. Without great Professional Sales Associates many stores would not remain in business.

Selling is not yelling or telling, it is helping

As a Professional Sales Associate you deal with each Customer as a unique human being. Customers do not "check" their personalities or problems before they come into a store. They come in as the sum total of all of their past experiences. That experience could be the fight they just had with their parents, children, or friends; the driver who cut them off in the parking lot; the other shopper who bumped them in the mall; and numerous other problems and irritations of the week, year or a lifetime. Customers also bring in expectations of what a certain product or service will do for their lives. They may expect a certain dress, TV or drill will transform their lives. Or they may just expect to find what they need and get home as soon as possible. There are millions of different motivations, moods and expectations you have to deal with as a Professional Sales Associate.

Dealing with human beings is one of the most complex jobs on earth. Every Customer is different, and even the

> **Dealing with human beings is one of the most complex jobs on earth.**

same Customer is different each time you see him or her. The complexities of trying to match a product with the needs of this very complex Customer is a challenge indeed. It requires that you not only have an excellent understanding of your product, but that you also have a thorough understanding of your Customer and his needs.

What makes a great Sales Associate?

Although it is true that great Sales Associates are made not born, there are some things that you must have inside you in order to become a great Sales Associate. The first is Ego. Selling is sometimes about rejection. There are Customers who, no matter how well you do your job, will reject what you are trying to sell them. Sometimes this rejection can be harsh: The Customer will be rude, angry, or just tell you that "your baby is ugly." The successful Sales Associate must have a healthy Ego; that allows this kind of rejection to be taken in stride. She or he must know that the rejection is not personal, but is rather the rejection of an idea or product. Although you can learn to deal with rejection, it is necessary to have a healthy Ego because knowing something intellectually is entirely different from knowing it emotionally. It is easy to say that my friend passed by me in the hall without saying hello because she was busy thinking about a test. But feeling in your gut that this is the real reason is not so easy. A Professional Sales Associate must therefore have a good, healthy view of her or himself.

The second trait that is critical for success in selling is empathy, the ability to understand another person's situation, feelings and motives. If you have empathy, you can better serve your Customers by being so in tune with them that you can often identify one of your products that will meet their needs. Empathy is not sympathy: You understand, but you do not feel sorry for your Customers.

The abundance of Ego and empathy makes for a great Sales Associate. They are the two secrets of good selling. Having these traits is not enough, however. You must learn how to use them in selling. Once you do, there will be no limit to how high you can go in your career or how much you can sell.

A brief history of selling

For thousands of years people have made the things that they need with their hands. If you needed a new pair of shoes 300 years ago, you would either have made it yourself from animal hide or bartered with a local craftsman to make a pair for you. The same was true for almost all goods. In the late 1800s the advent of the steam engine and other motors made the assembly line possible, which, in turn, led to the Industrial Revolution. For many years after almost all the goods that were produced in factories were bought by a public that was hungry for the products. It almost did not matter what the product was, there was a market for it.

As we advanced into the 20th century, and began producing more than was necessary, the modern salesman was born. I say salesman, because in the early days of selling almost all salespeople were men. The job of the early salesman was to sell what the factories produced. This selling was not concerned with what the Customer needed: It was only concerned with what the company had too much of and therefore had to push onto the Customer. The early salesman was characterized by having a "script" or a set sales "pitch" that was delivered to every Customer regardless of need. It is no wonder that salesmen soon got a reputation of being pushy.

It did not take long for Hollywood, the media and others to portray the job of selling as something not quite honest or honorable. Our society is rife with jokes about salesmen. Movies also often portray selling as a questionable profession. You may have seen *Death of a Salesman*, a play and movie about a salesman. It is a very harsh and critical portrayal of a salesman that may reflect the truth of the '50s, but not the '90s. You may also have seen the modern-day look at salespeople in the movie *Cadillac Man*, with Robin Williams, or the portrayal of the two extremes of stereotypical salespeople in *Pretty Woman*. In *Pretty Woman* we see two distinctly different portrayals of Sales Associates, neither of which is very accurate. One scene has two very haughty women ask, "May I help you?" when Julia Roberts enters the store. They then proceed to shame her out of the store. This is the Sales Associate as snob. In the second store scene, we see the overzealous store manager groveling at the feet of Richard Gere. This is the Sales Associate as slave.

By these portrayals, Hollywood would have us believe that only two types of Sales Associates exist. While there may still be some pushy salespeople in stores, they are often just poorly trained individuals who have not been exposed to proper selling techniques.

Marketing selling

In the late 1950s the concept of Marketing selling took root. By this time the factories of the world were producing more than enough products for everyone's needs. The old product push was not working as well anymore, and companies had to find a way to sell more products. Marketing selling defines success as discovering what the Customer's needs are and matching your product to those needs. Brilliant! This is the kind of selling that has taken over the old style of push selling. Marketing-driven selling is what the Professional Sales Associate practices and is what this book is all about.

You need to treat each Customer as you would like to be treated yourself.

The Golden Rule

The American Heritage Dictionary defines a friend as: 1. A person whom one knows, likes, and trusts. 2. A person whom one knows; an acquaintance. 3. A person with whom one is allied in a struggle or cause; a comrade.

As a Professional Sales Associate you will find the way you treat your Customers is very similar to the way you treat your friends. This is not to say you have to like every one of your Customers, but you do have to show them respect, consideration and overwhelming concern for their well-being.

The Golden Rule applies to selling almost more than any other profession. You need to treat each Customer as you would like to be treated yourself. You see, everything that you become, all that you will own and have, comes from your Customers. From the clothes on your back, to the roof over your head, to the food you eat — all are results of your Customer buying from you. A successful Sales Associate realizes this very important truth. If every Customer is responsible for your income and well-being, you should treat every Customer accordingly.

This is often easier said than done. When was the last time anyone who waited on you in a store gave you the feeling that you were that important to them? Yet, would you mistreat the person responsible for your income? A Professional Sales Associate knows that the Customer really is Number One. She treats him that way every day.

As a Professional Sales Associate, you need to form a deep commitment to helping others before you can be successful in selling. Your success is a direct result of a Customer's satisfaction, and that satisfaction is a direct result of your professionalism and commitment to the Customer. The two are inseparable. No Sales Associate can be successful without meeting the needs of his Customers, and no Customer will continue to buy from a Sales Associate who does not satisfy her needs.

Your success is a direct result of a Customer's satisfaction...

Vending machine selling

In this book I make the distinction between Professional Sales Associates and clerks. Clerks are Jerks. Clerks are like coin slots on vending machines: You just put your money in and out comes a product. A vending machine cannot answer a question, provide critical product knowledge, keep you from making a mistake, really understand your needs, and find the best product to meet those needs. A vending machine is just there to take money. Professional Sales Associates have careers: Clerks have jobs. Professional Sales

Associates build businesses: Clerks care-take businesses. Professional Sales Associates build relationships with Customers: Clerks take money from Customers. This book is for people who want to be Professional Sales Associates, not clerks.

The nine steps to a successful sales relationship

Although the following are listed as "steps", they are also stages that you go through *with* your Customer. The steps are:

1. The Greeting (Opening)
2. Needs Determination
3. Product Knowledge (Features, Attributes and Benefits)
4. Adding Value By Trading Up
5. Suggestion Selling
6. Answering Objections
7. The Close
8. Maximizing the Last Moment
9. Providing After Sales Services

Each chapter of this book will explain each step and give you practical exercises to help develop your skills.

The sales road map

Every journey has a best route. The best route is the one that brings you to your destination in the most efficient and enjoyable manner. A sale is a journey. It is not a desti-nation. As a Professional Sales Associate you must recognize that a sale is not a one-time event, but rather a stop-over point in your relationship with a Customer. The actual sale consists of a series of steps that you must follow to ensure that you are doing your job correctly, that is, pleasing your Customer.

Not every sale has all nine steps. Some sales will contain only four, while others will have six or seven. No sale should ever contain less than four of the steps. Even that Customer who runs into the store, knows exactly what she needs, grabs it, races up to the cash register and pulls out her wallet to pay, still deserves at least four of the steps of a good sale. You will soon see why.

Practice

As with learning any new skill, practice is the key to success. But often when we first try something new, it just does not feel right. That's because we are creatures of habit and often feel more comfortable doing something the way we always have. I would like you to take a moment, put down the book and try something.

Cross your arms. That's right, just cross your arms the way that you usually do. Now, uncross them and reverse them. If you had your left arm over right, then put your right arm over left. How does it feel? Probably, pretty strange. We are in the habit of crossing our arms a certain way, just as we are in the habit of doing a million things a certain way. Whenever we change that tried and true way, it feels uncomfortable.

... a sale is not a one-time event, but rather a stop-over point in your relationship with a Customer.

This book will make you do some things that at first will feel uncomfortable, but with practice will eventually become second nature. With these changes, you will be selling better and making more Customer/Friends than you ever thought possible. You will soon begin to recognize how difficult this journey will be and how much you will need to learn in the process. Brain surgery will begin to look simple by comparison!

KEEP IN MIND:

➤ Dealing with human beings is one of the most complex jobs on earth.

➤ Marketing selling defines success as discovering what the Customer's needs are and matching your product to those needs.

➤ Treat each Customer as you would like to be treated yourself.

➤ Your success is a direct result of a Customer's satisfaction, and that satisfaction is a direct result of your professionalism and commitment to the Customer.

➤ Not every sale will have all nine steps.

➤ A sale is not a one-time event, but rather a stop-over point in your relationship with a Customer.

Chapter 1

Step One
The Greeting

···

(Also known as
The Opening)

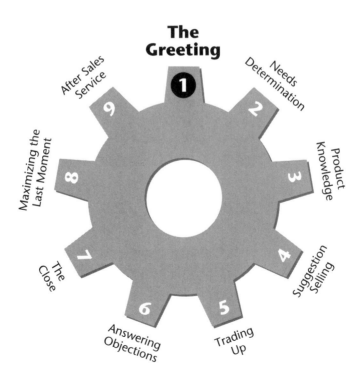

> Men greet each other with a sock on the arm, women with a hug, and the hug wears better in the long run.
>
> *Edward Hoagland, U.S. novelist, essayist*

Every sale begins with the greeting, yet this is the step at which most sales are lost. Your only job at this step is to welcome the Customer and make sure that she or he knows you work in the store. That is all you have to do at this step. You do not have to determine the Customer's needs, but just welcome him or her.

"May I help you?"

Very often we hear, "May I help you?" as a greeting to open the sale. This is a major mistake for a number of reasons.

What is the question, "May I help you?" really asking? I would suggest that it is a needs determination question. "Why are you here?" would be a more appropriate question, yet it would not sound right in a store setting. "May I help you?" ignores the Greeting and jumps right to Step Two, needs analysis.

Let me put it this way. Have you ever invited people over for dinner? You probably told them what time to come and that they really did not need to bring anything. As you were preparing dinner, the doorbell rang. Did you go to the door, open it up and immediately ask, "What would you like to drink?"

I don't think so. You probably opened the door and said, "Hi, it's great that you could come. Please, come right in." After gathering their coats and getting them seated in the living room, you probably then asked, "Can I get you something to drink, or would you like something to nibble on?"

What you did was to greet your guests, and once they were comfortably seated, analyze their needs. The same applies to your store. You first greet the Customer and make them feel comfortable, then you determine their needs.

What type of greeting is the best?

Often, the simplest greeting is the best. Your only job during the opening is to make the Customer comfortable and to let him know that you work in the store. Sometimes a simple "Hi" is sufficient. Some Sales Associates are more comfortable with a more formal, "Good Morning" or "Good Afternoon." What is important, is that you feel comfortable with the greeting and that the greeting is *not* a question that can be answered with a yes or no.

The greeting should also reflect the feeling or mood of your store. You would probably not say "Hi" if you work in a very expensive store. "Good Afternoon" would be more appropriate.

The reason that we do not want to ask a "yes or no" question at the opening is to avoid a "no" answer. It is always hard to maintain contact with the Customer after he has said no to a question. Even such pleasant openers such as, "It's a nice day, isn't it?" are risky. You will undoubtedly confront the tired or grumpy Customer who will respond, "NO!" You will then have to back off.

The other reason for not asking, "May I help you?" is that most Customers respond, "No thanks, I am just looking." How many times has this happened to you when you were a Customer? Then a few minutes later, when you really did have a question or need help, the Sales Associate was nowhere to be found.

The "Like me" bias

Sometimes we, as humans have a tendency to more comfortably approach people who are "like us" more easily than those who are not like us. "Like us" means of the same ethnic, social, age and gender group. There are some exceptions to this tendency, such as an older female associate who approaches a younger Customer in a "motherly" way, and a younger Sales Associate who approaches an elderly Customer as a grandchild would. The danger is when we approach a Customer who is not like us. We need to be very aware of our thoughts and not prejudge the Customer in any way. We cannot assume that the Customer does or does not have money, or that the Customer will respond or react a certain way. Remember: Every Customer, every human is different. The more we are aware of our tendency to prejudge or categorize people, the better able we will be to avoid doing it. If there is one thing I have learned as a Professional Sales Associate, it is that first impressions of people are wrong as often as they are right, probably more often wrong than right!. Treat every Customer as a potential million dollar Customer, and you will never go wrong.

Treat every Customer as a potential million dollar Customer and you will never go wrong.

How Customers behave

It is important to realize that every Customer who comes in your store has taken a risk to do so. It may not be the heart stopping, bungee jumping type of risk, but rather the psychological risk of entering a space that is not familiar. Even with this mild sense of risk, the Customer is on guard against what is happening around him. If you rush up to a Customer who has just entered the store, you will frighten him. Again, it is not the type of fear that stops hearts or raises blood pressure, but it is apprehension. The smart Sales Associate will recognize this response in his Customer and will be very sensitive to the first approach.

Try this experiment in your store. When a Customer comes in the store, walk towards her and say, "Hi." How did the Customer respond? In most cases the Customer will say, "No, I am just looking." Although you did not say, "May I help you?", that is precisely what the Customer heard. You see, Customers have become like Pavlov's Dog (that famous experiment in conditioning of response) and often respond to the greeting of the Sales Associate as if she had really asked the dreaded question. The act of walking toward a Customer is enough of a "threat" to stop her from hearing what you really said.

Try another approach. To the next Customer who comes in the store, rather than walk toward her, take a step *backwards* (make sure that you are not standing near any stairs!) and say, "Hi." What you will hear back, in almost every case is a "Hi." from the Customer. Why did she all of a sudden hear what you actually said? What was different?

The answer is your body language. In not physically approaching the Customer in those first few seconds, the Customer did not feel threatened in any way. She was therefore comfortable enough to really hear what you said. Although this may not work with every Customer (there are a few who are so deeply conditioned that they will say, "No, I am just looking." no matter what), in the vast majority of cases it will prove successful.

Ideal distance

The ideal distance from the Customer at the approach stage is about 15–25 feet. This is not always possible — you may be working at the front of the store when a Customer comes in the door, and you certainly should not start running backwards to get 25 feet away. But you should be sensitive to the personal space of the Customer and make sure that you are giving him a good distance so that he will not feel threatened. Elderly Customers are particularly sensitive to fast approaches, probably due to past experiences with clerks. Just remember: Do not physically approach the Customer during the greeting. As you progress into the sale and the relationship with the Customer, the distance you maintain will decrease. At each step I will define for you the ideal distance.

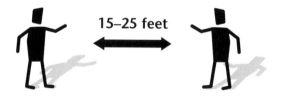

Practice

What is the best greeting for you? Choose a relatively standard greeting that you feel comfortable with so that you are never tempted to fall back on the old standby, "May I Help You?" The simplest is the best. A nice "Hi" works for most people. Write down three greetings that you feel comfortable with and that do not contain a question. You are not determining needs yet, and you do not want to risk a "no" answer from the Customer during the opening. Try your greetings with some Customers who come in the store. See which one you feel most comfortable with, as well as the one to which Customers respond the best. Also listen to other Sales Associates when you are a shopper. Try to pick up some new ideas for greetings. When you hear a great one, remember it.

My openers are:

_____

_____

_____

Remember:

☐ They cannot be answered with a yes or no

☐ They reflect a positive attitude to the Customer

☐ They are honest and comfortable

☐ They reflect the feeling of the store

KEEP IN MIND:

➤ You should feel comfortable with the greeting that you use, and it should *not* be in the form of a question that can be answered with a yes or no.

➤ First impressions of people are probably more often wrong than right.

➤ Treat every Customer as a potential "Million Dollar Customer", and you will never go wrong.

➤ Do not physically approach the Customer the first few seconds after he has entered your store, to avoid threatening him.

Chapter 2

Step Two
Needs Determination

Now that you have greeted the Customer and made
her feel welcome, it is time to move to Step Two and
discover her needs.

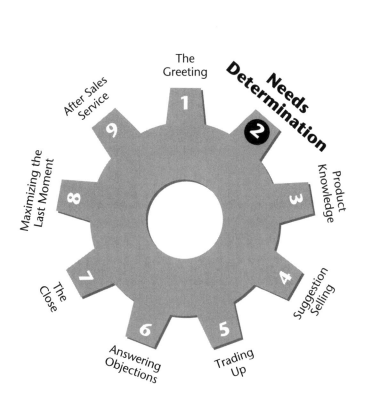

> # One of the best ways to persuade others is with your ears — by listening to them.
>
> *Dean Rusk (b. 1909), U.S. Democratic politician*

Why do Customers buy?

Customers usually do not go into stores just to get out of the rain (although, rarely they might!). They enter stores in search of something. The second step in your journey to the perfect sale is determining what a Customer really needs. The key words are *really needs*. Your job is to take what the Customer tells you and translate that into a product or service that will satisfy and delight the Customer. Here is an old story I heard in Marketing 101 in University which will give you some idea of what I am talking about.

A Customer goes into a hardware store and asks to see a drill. But is it a drill she really needs, or a hole? What should she have asked for?

Likely, her real need is a hole. Yet, can you imagine this Customer asking the Sales Associate for a two-inch deep three-eights of an inch hole?! The Sales Associate would think the Customer was nuts. But the Customer asked for a drill, not a hole. Did her request reflect her need?

Maybe not! Can you think of a reason why?[3] What questions might you ask this Customer to learn more?

---

[3] Possibly the Customer needs to turn screws and not drill holes. Therefore an electric screwdriver would be a better choice. Can you think of others?

Here are some questions that will give you insight into Customer needs. The answers are in the appendix of the book. Don't cheat! Answer the questions, and then look at the appendix to see how you did.

True/False

1. Customers usually know what they want. _____

2. Most Customers want to be left alone when shopping. _____

3. Many people buy when they are unhappy. _____

4. Customers cannot be persuaded to buy something they said they did not want. _____

5. In times of tight money, Customers buy only what they need. _____

6. What Customers ask for is not always what they want. _____

7. Most Customers have a price limit on their shopping needs. _____

8. Yesterday's luxuries are today's necessities. _____

9. Shopping can be an emotionally rewarding experience. _____

10. Spending money makes people happy. _____

How do I move from the Greeting to the Needs Determination stage?

1. Observe

2. Question

3. Listen between the lines

4. Suggest

Once you have greeted the Customer, then what do you do? Generally your best strategy at this point is to do nothing! Just observe what the Customer does. In most cases one of two things will happen:

A. The Customer will approach you and ask if you have a particular item or where an item can be found in the store; or,

B. The Customer will move to a particular area of the store and begin to look at merchandise.

It is rare that a Customer will just stop in the middle of the store and stare at the ceiling. Either the Customer will ask if you have something, or she will begin to look around. If she asks for a specific item, it is often best to answer her question with a question, particularly if you do not have that exact item in your store.

Let me give you an example:
A Customer enters the store and, after saying hi to you, asks you if you carry Arrow shirts. Unfortunately your store does not stock this brand of shirt. You could say to the Customer, "No, we do not carry Arrow shirts," upon which the Customer will likely turn and walk out of the store. Or you could try this approach. The Customer asks you if you carry Arrow shirts and you respond, "Oh, are you looking for a shirt for yourself or as a gift for someone?" This response does not have the Customer leaving the store, but instead gets her to talk to you. You answer the question with a question, because you do not have the specific requested merchandise and need to know more about this Customer's needs.

If the Customer was to ask for Arrow shirts and you did not carry shirts at all, of course you would let the Customer know. But if the Customer is looking for a shirt, you need to determine how important the Arrow brand is to the Customer before you walk away from her. By asking the "gift or yourself" question, you get the Customer talking and thereby have the chance to really determine if Arrow is important to the Customer or not. It is entirely possible this Customer is only marginally interested in Arrow as a brand and just thinks that Arrow is what she should be looking for. Or she could be using Arrow as a generic name for brand name shirts. As a Professional Sales Associate, you know you have many shirts in your inventory that are equal to, or better than, Arrow. However, if you just answer "no" to the Arrow question, you will lose the chance to show the Customer any shirts.

The quality of your first questions to the Customer is important, not only to maintaining the relationship with the Customer, but also in ensuring that you can match the right product to her needs by really determining what those needs are.

Open-ended questions

It is a good idea that all questions during the Needs Determination step be Open-ended Questions. Open-ended Questions are simply questions that cannot be answered with a yes or no or a one word answer. Remember, your job at this step is to learn as much as you can about the Customer's needs. You need to talk about 10 percent of the time (asking questions), and the Customer should be talking about 90 percent of the time. Closed questions such as, "Is this a gift?" are often answered with "no." This ends or makes it difficult to continue the conversation. Open-ended Questions, such as, "Tell me a little something about the person that the gift is for" or "How exactly do you want to use it?" or "How do you feel about this style?", are answered with more information by the Customer. In order to be effective, you need to be prepared. A Professional Sales Associate develops an entire list (repertoire) of questions she has memorized and has immediately available for use.

> **It is a good idea that all questions during the Needs Determination step be Open-ended Questions.**

When determining your Customer's needs, think about your merchandise. Begin by selecting a really popular item you sell quite a few of each week. It might be a blouse, a dinnerware set, a hammer, a watch — any product with which you are familiar. Ask yourself, what kind of Customer is generally interested in this kind of product. Is it important that the Customer be married, young, a college graduate or earn above a certain income? Should she have children or own a home? Will she be going to a party or attending school? What are some of the key things that would enable you to better sell the benefits of the product?

This takes a great deal of practice. At first, asking the questions will seem unnatural, not like you. Over time, however, you will acquire an easy style in asking the questions.

Nothing will leave my store until I know what it is for

Questions are critical in understanding the real needs of the Customer. If your commitment to the customer is to make sure that you fulfill her needs, then you also must make the commitment to the idea that, "Nothing will leave my store, until I know what it is for." What you are promising the Customer is that, as a Professional, you will sell her only what she needs. You cannot do this unless you take the time to really uncover and understand those needs.

Listen between the lines

Do you know the average human can process about 950 words per minute? And the average human can speak at about 150 words per minute? What do you think happens when we are listening to someone who is talking at 150 words per minute, and we have all that space left over? In most cases, we use this leftover space to think of other things: what we are going to say back to the person, what we are going to do that night, how we are going to find time to count all that stock that just came in. We seldom have problems filling up the space between people's words. It's the other things that we are thinking that often distract us from what others are saying. Have you ever been told by a friend in a conversation, "But I just told you that!" and you honestly did not hear it?

As a Professional Sales Associate you must become an excellent, active listener. This means that you become aware of your poor listening skills and actively engage your mind with the Customer. Here is one simple exercise that you can do with a friend or co-worker to help you understand the difference:

Speak a single simple sentence, with a question in it, to your friend. For example, you could say, "I had a tough time getting up for work today. I was exhausted. How about you?" Have your friend repeat your sentence word for word, then have her reply to it and add her own question. Then you repeat her reply, before you can answer her question. After several attempts, you will get some idea of how difficult it is to truly listen to everything that is being said. Generally as someone is talking to us, we are either busy formulating a reply or we are off in another world. Yet to satisfy your Customer's needs, you must hear those needs. The average person can listen to a 15 minute talk that is of great interest to her and, 10 minutes after the talk, only remember about 10 percent of what was said. Imagine how much we remember if it was boring!

What you are promising the Customer is that as a Professional you will sell him only what he needs.

Yet every Customer you meet has the right to your undivided attention. This is where active listening comes in. Practice repeating what the Customer says to you, in your head, while the Customer is talking, and at the same time, try to formulate questions that will give you more information about that Customer's needs. Use those extra

800 words per minute, which your brain has available to actively reflect on what the Customer is saying. It is as if you were a detective charged with investigating a crime, but in this case the only crime that might be committed is failure to meet the Customer's needs.

There are not a lot of books available on active listening, though there are some college courses that cover the basics. See what is available in your local area and sign up for any course that promises strategies for better communication skills. The more time you spend in discovering and uncovering others' needs, the easier the sale will be. The best needs determination leads to the best sales.

Running it up the flagpole

When attempting to learn more about your Customer's needs, it is not a bad idea to show your Customer an item and get her reaction to it. This is called, "running it up the flagpole and seeing who salutes" or "running it up the antenna to see what the reception is". Whatever you call it, suggesting or showing an item at this stage can often help you get information from your Customer. It is as important to know what he does not want, as what he does want.

When you show an item, watch and listen to your Customer very closely. Learn from what she both says and does not say. Also, observe her expressions. If a Customer bursts out laughing or frowns at a certain product, that should tell you something. Remember, the suggestion technique is only used after you have exhausted your questions and are not getting any more information from the Customer. But be careful, sometimes Customers will interpret suggesting items as pushiness. Keep in mind that you are still relatively early into your relationship with the Customer, and the last thing you want to do is pressure her.

The best needs determination leads to the best sales.

How Customers behave

The move from the Greeting to the Needs Determination step is a gentle one. Be aware that although you may now move closer to the Customer, do not rush towards her. Also be aware that people often say things they really do

People often need time to get used to a new idea.

not mean. How many times have you said something and regretted it a moment later? Things like, "I will never go out with you again!" or "I hate you!" or "That's the wrong color." Although we can often admit we have said something we did not mean, when another person tells us something, we usually assume it's the absolute truth.

For example, sometimes a Customer will reject an item or price the first time she hears it or sees it. Have you ever gone shopping, seen an item and rejected it because it was too expensive or the wrong color and then, after seeing other items, came back to the first and realized by comparison it was not very expensive or that the color was fine? Once you realize people often say things they may not mean, you will not make the mistake of rejecting an item that the Customer first responds to indifferently or negatively.

This is also related to a second truth about human behavior: People often need time to get used to a new idea. A Professional Sales Associate knows this and realizes, if she suggests an item to a Customer and the Customer rejects that item, it is not necessarily totally rejected. Customers can, and often do, change their minds. As a Professional equipped with this knowledge, when you hear the Customer say, "I don't like that color." or "That's the wrong style." or "That's much more than I wanted to spend.", you realize that the Customer can easily change her mind about this later in the sale. So do not make a big deal of it. Do not emphasize the point — it will only lead to the Customer solidifying this thought in her mind. If you gloss over this apparent rejection early in the sale, you will be able to re-introduce the item later, without making the Customer feel that she cannot go back on what she said earlier. (This is entirely different from an objection at the end of the sale, which I discuss later in the book. You would never gloss over an objection at that point in the sale.)

Once again, people will say things they really do not mean, and people will take time to get used to a new idea. During the needs analysis stage, therefore, listen very care-fully to what you are hearing and filter out what you, as the Professional, know may be caused by these two very human factors. You can and will often need to change the Customer's first thoughts and impressions during the sale.

Ideal distance

The ideal distance from the Customer during the Needs Determination stage is about five to 10 feet. Any closer, and the Customer will feel that you are "on their shoulder" and pushing them. Any further, and it is hard to carry on a conversation. If you are "running it up the flagpole", you will have to be closer to the customer. Obvious exceptions to this rule would be if you were in a jewelry store showing a customer a ring or small item when you would need to be closer to do this. Remember the rules, but never forget common sense!

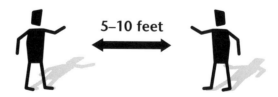

Practice

The most important part of determining needs is the questioning of the Customer during this stage. Have a standard set of questions that apply to each type of Customer who approaches any area of your store. Choose a particular display or presentation area in your store and imagine a Customer standing in front of this area. Write down three open-ended questions (questions that cannot be answered yes or no). The questions cannot be social — they must lead to information about the needs of the Customer.

For example, if I worked in a computer store and the Customer were looking in the hardware area at printers, I could ask, "Is most of your printing, business letters or do you print a lot of graphics?" Or "What kind of computer do you own?" The answer to either of these questions will give me more information about the Customer that will allow me to match a printer to her needs. Do not ask questions that do not give you product-relevant information. If it is not important that the Customer has children, then do not ask. If it is relevant, then ask. Eventually you should have questions for every area of your store.

Area of store: _____

Open-ended Question I would ask: _____

_____

Open-ended Question I would ask: _____

_____

Area of store: _____

Open-ended Question I would ask: _____

_____

Open-ended Question I would ask: _____

_____

KEEP IN MIND:

➤ Take what the Customer tells you and translate that into a product or service that will satisfy and delight the Customer.

➤ If a customer asks for a specific item, it is often best to answer her question with a question, particularly if you do not have that exact item in your store.

➤ The quality of your first questions to the Customer is important not only to develop a relationship with the Customer, but also to ensure that you can match the right product to her needs by really determining what those needs are.

➤ All questions during the Needs Determination step should be open-ended Questions.

➤ You need to talk about 10 percent of the time (asking questions), and the Customer should be talking about 90 percent of the time.

➤ What you are promising the Customer is that, as a Professional, you will sell her only what she needs.

➤ The best Needs Determination leads to the best sales.

➤ Be careful, sometimes Customers will interpret suggesting items as pushiness.

➤ People often say things they really do not mean.

➤ People often need time to get used to a new idea.

➤ Have a standard set of questions that apply to each type of Customer who approaches any area of your store.

➤ Remember: *Nothing will leave my store until I know what it is for.*

Chapter 3

Step Three
Product Knowledge

Now that you have determined the Customer's needs, it is time to take what you have learned and move to Step Three. At this step, you will match the Customer's needs to the knowledge that you have about your products. Some of this matching has already taken place in Step Two, as you actively listened to him and were already selecting the best suited product for him.

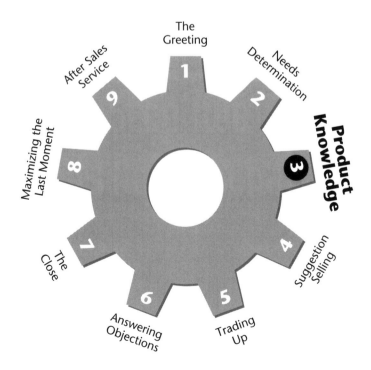

A man can only attain knowledge with the help of those who possess it. This must be understood from the very beginning. One must learn from him who knows.

George Gurdjieff (c. 1877–1949), Greek-Armenian religious teacher, mystic

The only way to be truly successful in selling is to match your Customer's needs to the specific performance or look of your product. After you have learned what your Customer's needs are, you must identify the features and attributes of your products that will meet the Customer's needs. Learn everything you can about your merchandise — you never know when a small detail you have discovered will make the difference in a sale.

Generally there is very little time in which to do this. It is an ongoing challenge. It means learning everything there is to know about each item in your store: How it was made, what it will and will not do, and most importantly, how it meets the needs of a specific Customer. For most Professional Sales Associates the acquisition of product knowledge takes up about 10 percent of the work day.

Features, attributes and benefits

Features, attributes and benefits of products are components so closely linked that Sales Associates refer to them as "FAB."

The features of a product are those things we can see, touch, smell, taste or hear. In other words, features are what are immediately obvious to our senses. They are concrete and directly observable and, therefore, noticeable by the Customer. The crystal a glass is made of, and the silk fabric of a blouse are features.

The attributes of a product are what the features do. Crystal makes a glass thin and delicate and provides a very clear surface. Silk is soft to the touch and "breathes," allowing air both in and out. Those are its attributes.

Features and attributes, however, do not sell a product nor do they pique a Customer's interest. Benefits do that. Demonstrating the benefit of a product involves taking the product's features and attributes and explaining, not just what they do, but what they can do *for* your Customer. In other words, the benefit statement means translating an attribute (what the product does) into a *personal* statement of what the product can do for your Customer.

A benefit statement always evokes the Customer's enjoyment or gain from the product.

For example, it is one thing to say that a coat is made of wool. It is another to add that wool is the warmest of natural fibers. But to say this wool coat will make you think you are in Miami on a warm day makes the Customer feel the warmth of the coat in a very real manner.

Just as seemingly natural greetings need to be practiced, so, too, do benefit statements. Always ask yourself if what you are saying to the Customer is a benefit to him or merely an explanation of the feature. A benefit statement always evokes the Customer's enjoyment or gain from the product. A benefit statement tells the Customer how this product will change his life. It personalizes the feature for the Customer and allows him to see how the product will make a difference in his life. Benefit statements almost always end in a description of the Customer enjoying, or getting something out of, the product.

F eatures are what we can see.

A ttributes are what features do.

B enefits are what features and attributes do for *the Customer* (as related to his or her *expressed* need).

Where do you begin to learn about your products?

Customers never buy features, they only buy what those features will do for them (benefits). Not only must you learn about the features and attributes of every item in your store, but you must also learn the benefits of each item as it relates to each Customer.

Begin by drawing on all our sources of product knowledge: your own experience with the merchandise, the buyer's and store manager's input, labels, tags, brochures, and product inserts. Handle, use or wear the merchandise. Read magazines and catalogs, and listen to the experiences of other Sales Associates and Customers. Ask suppliers' sales representatives questions about the products when they are in the store, or call or write them with questions. All of these are ways of acquiring more information about your products.

> **Customers never buy features, they only buy what those features will do for them.**

Product Knowledge

Product knowledge comes from:

- your own experience with the merchandise
- the buyer and store manager

- labels, tags, brochures and product inserts
- handling, using or wearing the merchandise
- magazines and catalog
- other Sales Associates and Customers
- Suppliers' sales representatives
- asking questions and talking about the merchandise

How Customers behave

As you move to match your product knowledge with the Customer's needs, you will be approaching the Customer to demonstrate or show your product to him. Realize that at this early stage, some Customers are still somewhat wary of committing to the process and may start to back away, refuse to hold the item or simply stop answering questions. If you notice a change in your Customer's behavior during this step, slow down and back up slightly to give him some room to move. Remember, it is still early in the sale, and the Customer does not yet have a high degree of trust in you.

Romancing your product

How you hold and present the merchandise will speak volumes to the Customer about how you feel about your product. Remember to treat each piece of merchandise as if it were a million dollar vase. If you show respect and care for the merchandise, the Customer will also appreciate the quality of the item and your store. If you are demonstrating the durability of an item, and it requires some rough handling, do it with precision and care. Customers will judge both you and your merchandise through subtle signals you give during this stage. If you are holding a garment, treat it as if it were worth one hundred times its tagged price. If it is a household item, handle it as you would an antique.

Ideal distance

The ideal distance during the Product Knowledge step is anywhere from three to five feet. While you will have to move closer to demonstrate the product or to put it into the Customer's hands, watch how close you are, and do not stand too close for a long period of time. If you are demonstrating something, it's not a bad idea to show it to the Customer, and then back up a step or two so the Customer will not feel pressured while he is examining it.

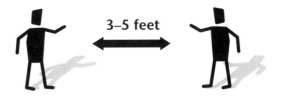

3–5 feet

Practice

Pick a Customer type that you now have, for example, a young married woman, a young single man, a student or an elderly man. Then select a product that you now sell in your store. Write down all the observable features of that product. Beside them, write the product's attributes — what each of the features actually does. In the last column, write the benefits for your chosen Customer type. Check that the benefits answer the question, "Why should the Customer care?" for each of the features and attributes. Although not every Customer who fits this description will need all the features and benefits, it is critical that you know all you can.

Customer Type _____

Feature of product (What does the product look like?)	Attribute (What does the feature do?)	Benefit (How does the feature help the Customer?)

This list may need several more lines for some products. Eventually you should have a list for every product or type of product you sell. The ability to listen to the Customer, hear his needs and select a feature and attribute that meet those needs in a matter of moments, is selling at its best. Only a true Professional Sales Associate can do this.

KEEP IN MIND:

➤ Learn everything you can about your merchandise — you never know when a small detail that you have discovered will make the difference in a sale.

➤ The features of a product are those things that we can see, touch, smell, taste or hear.

➤ The attributes of a product are what the features do.

➤ The benefit statement means translating an attribute (what the product does) into a *personal* statement of what the product can do for your Customer.

➤ A benefit statement always evokes the Customer's enjoyment or gain from the product.

➤ Customers never buy features: They only buy what those features will do for them (benefits).

➤ If you show respect and care for the merchandise, the Customer will also appreciate the quality of the item and your store.

Chapter 4

Step Four
Suggestion Selling

··

You have uncovered your Customer's needs and applied
the knowledge that you have about your product, and found
just the right product with features, attributes and benefits for
your Customer. Now you are ready to exceed his expectations
and suggest additional products that will enhance the
Customer's purchase.

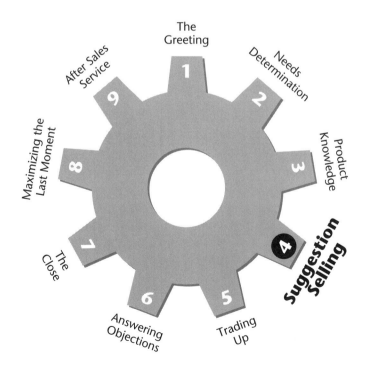

> To know how to suggest is the great art of teaching. To attain it, we must be able to guess what will interest; we must learn to read the childish soul as we might a piece of music. Then, by simply changing the key, we keep up the attraction and vary the song.
>
> *Henri Frédéric Amiel (1821–81), Swiss philosopher, poet*

The best Customer service

Are you the kind of person who is perfectly organized? You never forget anything, never miss an appointment, never leave something you needed at home? Do you know anyone who is perfectly organized? I don't.

Most people are not perfectly organized. In fact, most of us frequently forget things or neglect to do things when we should. Part of the job of a good Sales Associate is to protect your Customers from what I call "dented foreheads". Dented foreheads come from slapping your forehead while exclaiming, "Oh, I forgot to get, to do, to be...!"

Customers are generally rushed and preoccupied. More importantly, they do not have the information that you do about what would enhance the performance or look of the product they are buying. This is because you are the professional, and you have this information. A Customer may not even be aware, for instance, that there is a tie that goes with the shirt he wants to buy, or that he needs batteries to make his new clock work, or that by buying the accessory now, he will save himself a trip later. All of this is the job of the Professional Sales Associate.

You can also prevent the Customer from making the wrong decision or selecting the wrong item by suggesting properly. Since you know most Customers are not as expert in your products as you, it is your duty to help them make the right choice. If you can improve the performance or value of the item by selling an enhancement to the product, you do your Customer a service by simply pointing this out. Suggestion Selling is not pushy or improper: It is a true Customer Service only Professionals deliver. If more Sales Associates practiced Suggestion Selling, more Customers would be happier with their shopping experience.

This is because a Professional Sales Associate makes a difference in peoples lives. Sometimes those differences are minor, sometimes major. They are always significant, however. For example, think about the Customer to whom you sold a suit, and then took the extra time to suggest a complimentary shirt and tie. The next week, that Customer put that suit on for an important meeting. Because the Customer felt confident in the suit, he was able to make a very important contribution, during the meeting, which lead to a job promotion. Were you responsible for his job promotion? In part, yes. There lies the satisfaction in being a Professional Sales Associate.

> **Suggestion Selling is not pushy or improper: It is a true Customer Service that only Professionals deliver.**

How Customers behave

Believe it or not, most Customers respect and enjoy Suggestion Selling. When done properly, it is the gentle reminder that makes their life easier. You are not selling when you suggest, you are helping the Customer to remember something he forgot.

Ideal distance

The ideal distance for Suggestion Selling is about three to five feet. Suggestion Selling implies trust, and the distance to the Customer reflects this stage. You can now move closer to the Customer.

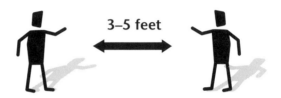

3–5 feet

Practice: The Twenty Dollar challenge

The next time you go out to buy something for yourself, try the following exercise. It will work best if you do it with a team of your fellow Sales Associates and all report back on the outcome. Here's what to do:

Take $20 with you and prepare to purchase an item that costs $10 or less. You can shop for film, lipstick, crayons, a paperback book or a hammer — whatever you happen to need that is ten dollars or less.

Enter the store with the $20 in your hand. As you select your chosen item, keep the twenty dollar bill in your hand, regardless of whether you are waited on by a Sales Associate or select it yourself. As you bring it up to the cash, either with a Sales Associate or alone, make sure that the twenty dollar bill is visible. If the cashier or Sales Associate asks you if there will be anything else, say "no." If, however, he asks you about a specific item to go with your purchase, such as batteries, mascara, a coloring book, another popular author's book or nails, immediately say "yes." If the Sales Associate (or clerk in this case) does not ask you about an additional item, allow him to complete the transaction and give you your change. Then ask him why he failed to suggest an additional item, such as batteries, mascara, a coloring book, another book or nails.

Write down his response once you have left the store. You will probably find responses such as:

- "If you wanted it, you would have asked for it."
- "It's not my job to suggest items."
- "I didn't think that you wanted anything else."
- Or my favorite, "Why should I bother, this job sucks."

The next step can be done by yourself or with a group of Sales Associates who have completed the same experiment.

How much change did you come out of the store with? How much would you have spent if you were asked? How many Customers do you think that store had that day?

Let's assume the store had 100 Customers that day, all of whom would have spent an additional $10 if they were just asked. Based on the estimate of 100 Customers a day, how much money went unspent that day? Answer: $1,000. When you take into account that the store is most likely open 360 days a year, how much money did that store potentially lose in lost opportunity? Answer: $360,000.

Even if every Customer would have spent only five dollars more, the additional business to the store would have totaled $180,000! Research[4] now tells us for every dollar spent in a store, the Customer would have spent another dollar if asked or encouraged.

---

[4] P.O.P. Institute Survey 1994

The Twenty Dollar Challenge

Fill in your own numbers:	
Amount to spend	$ _____
Amount spent	$ _____
Amount not spent	$ _____
Multiply amount not spent by number of Customers per day	_____
Equals total potential lost sales that day	= $ _____
Multiply by days store open	X _____
Total amount of potential lost business	$ _____

It should come as no surprise the amount of money that leaves a store every day. However, the total that you calculate above may astound you.

Improve Your Average Transaction

Set your own goal and exceed it!

My Scorecard for average transaction:

Week of _____	Average transaction goal	Actual average transaction	Percent above goal
Monday			
Tuesday			
Wednesday			
Thursday			
Friday			
Saturday			
Sunday			

KEEP IN MIND:

➤ Customers are generally rushed and preoccupied.

➤ Customers do not have the information you do about what would enhance the performance or look of the product they are buying.

➤ You can prevent a Customer from making the wrong decision or selecting the wrong item by suggesting properly.

➤ Suggestion Selling is not pushy or improper: It is a true Customer Service only Professionals deliver.

➤ Most Customers respect and enjoy Suggestion Selling

Chapter 5

Step Five
Trading Up

You have exceeded your Customer's expectations by
suggesting additional products that enhanced her selection.
Now you may want to go further by showing your best solution
to her needs. Not every Customer will need to be taken through
this step (you may have already shown the best item to her)
and some merchandise categories do not have a trade up
item that will apply.

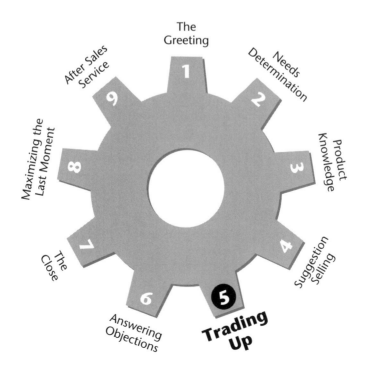

We can have in life but one great experience at best, and the secret of life is to reproduce that experience as often as possible.

Oscar Wilde (1854-1900), Anglo-Irish playwright, author

Show the best!

Every Customer has the right to be shown and sold the best. The trading up strategy is based on the principle that you usually get what you pay for. It is always a good idea to sell your Customers the best items that you have, because they will generally perform at the highest level, and the Customer will be happiest. This is no new concept. Over one hundred years ago, British social critic John Ruskin wrote:

> *It's unwise to pay too much, but it's worse to pay too little. When you pay too much, you lose a little money — that is all. When you pay too little, you sometimes lose everything, because the thing you bought was in-capable of doing the thing it was bought to do.*

> *The common law of business balance prohibits paying a little and getting a lot — it can't be done. If you deal with the lowest bidder, it is well to add something for the risk you run. And if you do that, you will have enough to pay for something better.*[5]

How many of us have learned this lesson by buying something that did not hold up to our expectations, or that fell apart soon after we used or wore it? A Professional Sales Associate will not allow this to happen to her Customer.

---

[5]   John Ruskin, 1885

Underselling

There is nothing worse than underselling a Customer. This happens when you do not spend the time necessary to discover the Customer's real needs or how long she needs an item to last. You can also fall prey to this habit if you do not truly believe in the value of your merchandise.

Above all, selling must be of the highest ethics and honesty. Do not sell a Customer an item that you know is defective or not worth the price you are charging. If you believe in your merchandise, then make sure that you sell your Customer the best. If you do not, the Customer will buy the cheaper item, and a few days or weeks later, it may break or fall apart. While the Customer will not remember that she paid three or five dollars less for the item, or blame the manufacturers, she will remember, "the lousy store that sold me this junk."

Needless to say, you cannot afford to have your Customers thinking of your store this way. If you show the best

There is nothing worse than under-selling a Customer.

product at the beginning of the sale, and let the Customer see the difference between the good, the better, and the best products, she most often will choose the better or the best one. When she chooses the better or best, you both win. She wins because she has selected something that will serve her well. She will also be happy with your store, and thus you will benefit from a satisfied Customer who comes back to you.

Think of it this way. Let's say you buy a $45 pair of pants, and they last 12 washings before they start to look worn. Then you buy a $60 pair of pants that last 24 washings. That $15 increase gave you twice the life of the first pair of pants for only 33 percent more money. But if you are not aware of this benefit (lack of product knowledge) and do not know that this is important to the Customer (lack of needs awareness), you can fail to point it out. The more you learn about your Customer, the easier it will be to exceed her expectations by selling her your very best products. The

Think in terms of selling right and not selling up or down.

opposite is equally true. If you know that your Customer will only require the use of the item once, or for a very brief time, it is imperative that you sell her the lower priced or lower quality item, as it will be discarded quickly, and the Customer should not pay for more than she needs. Think in terms of selling right and not selling up or down.

An increasing number of Customers today are responding to quality in products. Like never before, they are ready to pay extra money for a quality product, keeping in mind the old saying, "You get what you pay for." Quality does not come cheap. Yet as the example demonstrates, the price increase is often marginal compared to the increase in quality and durability of the better product. Yet no matter how much the durability increases, if it is not needed, then it should not be sold.

How Customers behave

Most Customers are in a great rush while shopping these days. They no longer have time to browse and examine products, as they did in the past. It is, therefore, very important that the Professional Sales Associate take the initiative and show the Customer the best solution to her needs. In almost every sale this means showing the Customer the best items first. If the Customer is going to make a quick decision, or is comparing products, then it is far better that she be urged to buy your best and experience the satisfaction that comes with it, than purchase the lower priced, poorer quality item that could lead to dissatisfaction.

Ideal distance

The ideal distance for trading a Customer up is three to five feet. Stand close enough to show or demonstrate the product, yet give the Customer space to inspect, think and make her decision.

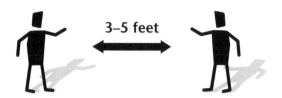

3–5 feet

Practice

Select a group of items from your store. They should be similar products and vary only in price. Pick items that offer a range of a low, moderate and high price. For example, you may have a 55 cent, 75 cent and one dollar chocolate bar. Even though all are made of the same ingredients, you get six ounces for 55 cents, nine ounces for 75 cents, and 14 ounces for one dollar. Can you come up with a reason why you should show the Customer the dollar candy bar first? What benefit does it have over the other two? In what case would you *not* try to sell the one dollar bar?

Select your items and list the prices below.

Quality	Item Name	Price
Good		
Better		
Best		

For the next week, whenever a Customer comes into your store looking for this item, try the following:

Greet the Customer and determine whether she needs this item. If she does, show her the best product first. If you are concerned about losing the sale because she will think that you only carry high priced merchandise, then show the better at the same time, or show the good with the best. Observe how the Customer looks at, and compares, the two products. Point out the features of the best product and let the Customer see how the good or better one does not have all of these features. Count how many times during the week you try this and count how many times the Customer buys each kind.

Number of Customers shown Best   _____

Number of sales of Good   _____

Number of sales of Better   _____

Number of sales of Best   _____

If you are like most Professional Sales Associates, you will find that you sell far more of the best, simply because it was shown to the Customer. Most Customers will buy a better product if they can see the difference, or have the difference it explained to them. After you have tried this exercise a few times, you will begin to show the best product to every Customer and only sell the best or better items. Remember, it is in the true interest of your Customer for her to purchase the best quality item you offer.

KEEP IN MIND:

➤ Every Customer has the right to be shown and sold the best.

➤ Sell your Customers the best items you have, because they will generally perform at the highest level.

➤ There is nothing worse than underselling a Customer.

➤ Do not sell a Customer an item you know is defective or not worth the price you are charging.

➤ If you show the best product at the beginning of the sale, and let the Customer see the difference between the good, the better, and the best products, she most often will choose the better or the best one.

➤ Think in terms of selling right and not selling up or down.

➤ Quality does not come cheap: The price increase is often marginal compared to the increase in performance and durability of the better product.

➤ In almost every sale, show the Customer the best items first.

➤ Most Customers will buy a better product if they can see the difference or have the differences explained to them.

Chapter 6

Step Six
Answering Objections

··

You went the extra step and showed your best solution to your Customer's needs. Most Customers are now ready to be sold and it is now time to move to the closing step. Some Customers may have a problem with the purchase and raise an objection at this point. In Step Six you learn how to answer objections.

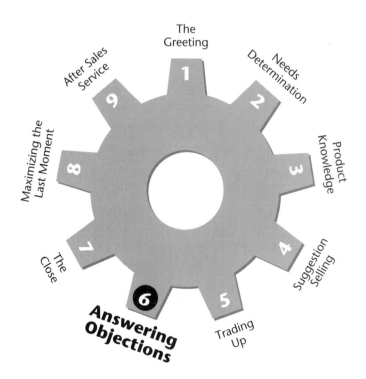

> A technical objection is the first refuge of
> a scoundrel.
>
> *Heywood Broun (1888-1939), U.S. journalist, novelist*

In some sales there comes a time when the Customer will voice an objection to the product. Sometimes an objection can cause you to lose a sale: Sometimes it can make the Customer nervous about the purchase. If you better understand objections, you can learn how to address them and ensure that they do not end a good sale. You will learn that most objections are not what they appear to be at first glance.

Objections need not end the sale

Objections are really the "breakfast of champions" to a Professional Sales Associate. They keep you from making the mistake of selling when you should not, and they give you valuable information about your Customer.

This said, most objections do not need to end the sale. Some objections result from poor communication on your part, and some are due to a lack of understanding or trust from the Customer. You must learn to tell the difference between the types of objections, so you can face them honestly and openly. Many sales are lost because the Sales Associate failed to properly answer an objection. Remember, an objection is not the rejection of the sale by a Customer — most often it is a cry for help, for more information or, simply, for reassurance.

Three steps to handling an objection

"I really like it, but it costs too much."

"I really wanted an all-wool sweater, not a cotton blend."

"I had my heart set on blue."

"I would buy it, but I don't believe that it will last the whole season."

When you first hear an objection like the ones above, immediately repeat the objection back to the Customer in your own words. You do this for three reasons:

First, you want to ensure that you really understand the objection. When you repeat the Customer's concern, some-times she will say, "No, I don't mean it costs too much. What I really mean is that I don't have enough money with me." In this case, you can recommend a lay-away (if your store has this policy) or suggest a deposit to hold the item.

When you first hear an objection like the ones above, immediately repeat the objection back to the Customer in your own words.

Second, by repeating the objection you are telling the Customer that you are concerned about her feelings. No Customer wants a Sales Associate to ignore her concerns.

Third, in repeating the objection, you give yourself a few valuable seconds to identify the exact nature of the objection and form the proper response.

Therefore, by repeating the objection you help clarify what the problem is, you reassure the Customer, and you give yourself time to respond properly. The first few times you do this, it will feel stilted. It does not feel natural to para-phrase a statement back to a person. Once you practice this a few times, however, it will feel very natural. (See the practice exercises at the end of this chapter.) After repeating the objection, the next step will depend on the nature of the objection.

Typical objections

- **Skepticism**
- **Confusion**
- **Perceived Drawback**

An objection due to skepticism

When the Customer does not believe something you have said about the product or the performance of the product, the objection is based on skepticism. The Customer is really saying, "I do not believe you." This disbelief could be due to a past experience she had with a similar product, something that she heard from a friend, or something she read about the product. Whatever the source of the skepticism, she is not going to buy until she believes the product is different from what she now understands it to be. Here are some examples of objections due to skepticism:

"I don't like this one. I had a shirt just like this and it shrunk in the wash."
"This can't be warm, it's too thin."
"I don't believe this will do all the thing you say it will."
"How can you guarantee this will work?"

Although skepticism is expressed in a variety of ways, you can always recognize it by the Customer's concern about the product's ability to perform. How do you handle this kind of objection? First, repeat the objection. Then offer proof.

Sound simple? It is, if you have proof. Proof is just what it sounds like: It is the evidence or argument that compels the Customer to accept an assertion as true. You cannot invent proof, and you cannot fake it. Proof must be based on your product knowledge, that is, your experience with the product, or the experience of your Customers. For most Professional Sales Associates gathering proof statements about products happens every day. If you buy and use the products you sell, then your personal experience with the product is, honest proof statement. Here is an example of a proof statement:

"So you're concerned that if you wash this shirt it will shrink? Well, I have the same shirt, and being the most forgetful person in the world, I put it in the hot wash by mistake and then in the dryer, and it didn't shrink an inch!"

Remember, you cannot make up proof; you either have it or you do not.

That is a real proof statement, and you can only use it if it is true. But what if you do not own the shirt, or own it but have never washed it? In this case, you can say, "So, you're concerned that if you wash this shirt it will shrink? I have sold lots of these shirts and have never had one returned because it shrank. As a matter of fact, some of my Customers have told me that it washed very well."

But what if you have never sold the shirt before and have no other Customer feedback? Here you can say, "So, you're concerned that if you wash this shirt it will shrink? I have read the specifications from the manufacturer, and they point out that they have changed the construction of the fabric and have pre-shrunk the fabric so that it is guaranteed not to shrink."

In each of these cases you are able to offer real proof to the Customer and can effectively sell the shirt.

But what if you do not own the shirt, do not know anyone who does nor have any manufacturer's specifications or literature? In short, what if you do not have proof that the shirt will not shrink? Simple: You will lose the sale. Too many sales are lost because the Sales Associate cannot prove to the Customer that the product does what the Customer wants it to. I suspect thousands of sales are lost this way each day. Remember, you cannot make up proof: You either have it or you do not. Make sure, therefore, that you spend time building your "proof library" for each product that you sell.

An objection due to confusion

When the Customer does not hear something you said about your product or misunderstands what you said, an objection due to confusion can arise. Such objections often sound like these:

"I wanted 100 percent cotton, not a blend."
"I thought that I could just put this in the dishwasher."
"I wanted one with four megs of RAM, not two."
"I wanted it to be machine washable."

Confusion is easily identified because it is based on a mistake the Customer has made. But before you set her straight, remember to repeat the objection back to her. You

> **Confusion is easily identified because it is based on a mistake the Customer has made.**

could say, "You wanted 100 percent cotton, not a blend? I am very sorry, I must have forgotten to tell you this is 100 percent cotton and not a blend." This may seem easier than it is, especially when you have told the Customer several times the product is all cotton. You may be tempted to say, "Are you deaf or what? I told you this was all cotton!" Needless to say, avoid such responses!

The key to handling an objection, due to confusion, is to clarify the misunderstanding by blaming yourself for poor communication. Because you are guiding the sale, it is generally your fault that the Customer did not understand properly the first time. Once again, when the Customer has misunderstood: repeat, take the blame, and clarify.

An objection due to a perceived drawback

When the Customer objects to something that is wrong with the product, the objection is based on a perceived drawback. The objection is not caused by doubt about what the product will do nor is it due to a misunderstanding. The Customer is objecting to a real problem with the product. This is the toughest objection that a Professional Sales Associate can handle. It is the type of objection that loses most sales. But it does not have to. In most cases, the perceived drawback objection can be overcome with knowledge and skill, and when done properly, is the mark of a real professional.

Do you own anything that is perfect? Do you have a "significant other" who is perfect? Is there nothing about your friends, parents or children that you would not change if you could? How about your favorite outfit? Wouldn't it be just that much better if it only...

None of us own perfect things or know perfect people. We all accept the negative aspects of things and people if the overall picture is positive. In fact, whether we know it or not, we tend to run a "balance sheet" for both things and people. We tally up what we like about something or someone and list them as "assets," and then list things we do not like as "liabilities." Take, for instance, that favorite pair of jeans that had the comfortable, soft feel and cool look. Those were its assets. But eventually the large hole in the rear end caused the liability side to outweigh the asset side, and it was time to throw the jeans out. As with all products, when the liabilities exceed the assets, we no longer use the item. In relationships, when the liabilities exceed the assets, we get a divorce!

What is essential to keep in mind, is that like all things and people in our lives, not every sale is perfect for the Customer. In many sales, the Customer identifies something that she does not like about the item — its liability. Your job is to determine if the liability outweighs the assets. In other words, is what the Customer finds objectionable about the item greater than all the things she likes about the item?

A perceived drawback is nothing more than liabilities overshadowing assets. A Customer may like many things about the product (its features and attributes) and may realize that these things are very important to her (benefits), but one part of the product she really does not care for may prevent her from appreciating the assets. Your job is to make sure that the Customer is not making a mistake by letting one dislike overshadow all the likes.

Early on in the sale, you determined your Customer's needs. If you did your job properly, you already know quite a bit about the Customer and have a more "objective"[6] viewpoint of his needs. The Customer, on the other hand, has a more subjective[7] or personal view. Your objectivity, along with your professional training, should make you a better judge of what is right for the Customer. This is not to say that you have the right to force a decision upon a Customer. What you need to realize, however, is that the Customer has expressed a need and you have the knowledge and experience to match that need with a fulfilling product. To have second thoughts about a purchase deci-

---

[6]   Objective means "Uninfluenced by emotions or personal prejudices." The American Heritage Dictionary of the English Language, Third Edition is licensed from Houghton Mifflin Company. Copyright © 1992 by Houghton Mifflin Company. All rights reserved.

[7]   According to the American Heritage Dictionary, subjective means that which is "taking place within a person's mind such as to be unaffected by the external world."

sion is normal and natural. No Customer wants to buy something that is useless or that will make him unhappy. A perceived drawback, therefore, is a cry for help. It is the Customer saying, "I am not sure this product is right for me." Your job is to test the reality of that statement and determine if it is just a case of the buyer's second thought, or if there truly is a liability that will seriously impact the Customer's use and enjoyment of the product.

No Customer wants to buy something that is useless or that will make him unhappy.

At the same time, however, it is very common for a Customer to talk herself out of something that is right for her. How many times have you found yourself saying, days or weeks after not buying an item, "I wish I'd bought that when I had the chance!" Your job is to ensure Customers never do this.

To properly handle an objection due to a perceived drawback, follow the first step of any objection, that is, say it back to the Customer. Here's an example:

Customer: I really don't want to pay more than $50 for a bowl.

Sales Associate: So you're concerned with paying more than your budget of $50 for this bowl?

Customer: Yes, I think it's too much to pay.

Sales Associate: I can certainly see why you feel that way. You had planned to spend at most $50, and now you are surprised at the $70 price. Well, I know that it appears to be over your budget, but you did like the color and said that it would be perfect in your kitchen. You also liked the fact that it can go from the freezer to the oven to the table and save you washing two extra bowls. You also liked the five year guarantee because the last bowl you had broken less than a year after you bought it. And remember, you said you use this kind of bowl about once a week. We calculated that over the minimum five year life of the bowl it would cost about 27 cents a week for the bowl. I really think, when you look at all you'll get from using this bowl — better color co-ordination, ease of use and serving, less dish washing time and a guarantee of a minimum of five years of use — you'll agree that the extra money is a wise investment.

This is an example of a classic method for overcoming an objection due to a perceived drawback. First, you repeat the objection to clarify it, and then show the Customer that you heard her. Second, you remind the Customer of all the benefits to which the Customer has already agreed. Finally, you summarize the benefits in an easy-to-understand manner that demonstrates to the Customer that all the assets (benefits) outweigh the small liability (price).

Not every objection due to a perceived drawback ends this happily. When you fail to develop a product's assets in the beginning of the sale, you may walk away from a "right" sale. But there are also times when a perceived drawback does, indeed, outweigh the benefits. Since the job of a Professional Sales Associate is to make it impossible for a Customer to make a mistake, in these cases you must stop the sale and prevent a bad purchase.

How Customers behave

"Cognitive dissonance" is a complicated term for buyer's remorse. Many Customers feel some remorse after making a purchase. Generally, the magnitude of the remorse or "dissonance" is in proportion to the cost of the purchase.

It is not unusual for people who buy cars to look in the paper for weeks afterwards, to make sure that the price has not gone down. Stereos, computers, furniture and other larger ticket items, in particular, trigger buyer's remorse. Buyer's remorse, however, is not inevitable. It can be reduced by the Sales Associate, by reassuring the Customer that she is making the right decision and you stand behind the product and the sale.

Ideal distance

The ideal distance for handling an objection is three to five feet from the Customer. Do not stand so close that the Customer feels like you are pressuring her. Nor should you be too far away. This is a time of indecision for the Customer, and she often needs reassurance. Maintain a comfortable distance, yet remain close enough to assure the Customer.

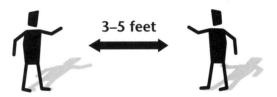

Practice

The best way to prepare yourself for objections is to practice responding to them in advance. Create a list of common objections that you hear in your store. Write down how you can respond to them. This is not an easy task, but the pay off in more sales makes it worth doing it.

Objection due to skepticism

Example:

Customer: I really don't think that this will stand up to heavy use.

Sales Associate: What you mean is that you think that it will fall apart if it is handled roughly?

Customer: Yes, it just seems too flimsy.

Sales Associate: I can see how you would feel that way, as it appears very delicate. But I can assure you that it will stand up to the toughest use. I have sold over twenty of them and have had Customers come back and comment on how well they stood up to some very tough handling.

Your example: Skepticism

Customer: _____

_____

_____

Your response (rephrase objection): _____

_____

_____

Your response (offer proof): _____

_____

_____

Objection due to confusion

Example:

Customer: I thought that this was made in Canada. I don't buy imports.

Sales Associate: What you're saying is that it is important that your purchase be Canadian made?

Customer: Yes, that's very important to me. I want to keep jobs here in Canada.

Sales Associate: I very much agree, and I have to apologize for not pointing out to you that this is 100 percent Canadian made.

Your example: Confusion or misunderstanding

Customer: _____

_____

_____

Your response (rephrase objection): _____

_____

_____

Your response (clear up misunderstanding): _____

_____

_____

Objection due to a perceived drawback

Example:

Customer: I really had my heart set on navy blue.

Sales Associate: The color navy is very important to you?

Customer: Yes it is. I really prefer navy.

Sales Associate: I realize that the color is important, however, you do really like the way this style fits you. You were also impressed with the fact that it is completely machine washable and will save you money on dry cleaning. And the color is very neutral and will go with almost all of your other accessories. I realize that navy is your first choice, but I think you'll have an impossible time finding another outfit that has so many good points as this one.

Your example: Perceived drawback

Customer: _____

_____

_____

Your response (rephrase objection): _____

_____

_____

Your response (stress the benefits already agreed to): _____

_____

_____

Make copies of these sheets and try to develop answers to the objections you hear most frequently. Practice will make it easier each time. Your Customers will thank you!

KEEP IN MIND:

➤ Objections are really the "breakfast of champions" to a Professional Sales Associate.

➤ Objections keep you from making the mistake of selling when you should not, and they give you valuable information about your Customer.

➤ Many sales are lost because the Sales Associate failed to properly answer an objection.

➤ Remember, an objection is not the rejection of the sale by a Customer — most often it is a cry for help, for more information or simply for reassurance.

➤ When you first hear an objection, immediately repeat the objection back to the Customer in your own words.

➤ By repeating the objection you help clarify what the problem is, you reassure the Customer, and you give yourself time to respond properly.

➤ When the Customer does not believe something you say about the product or its performance, the objection is based on skepticism.

➤ You cannot make up proof: You either have it or you do not.

➤ When the Customer does not hear something you said about your product or misunderstands what you said, an objection due to confusion can arise.

➤ The key to handling an objection due to confusion is to clarify the misunderstanding by blaming yourself for poorly communicating.

➤ A perceived drawback is the toughest objection a Professional Sales Associate can handle.

➤ With a perceived drawback, your job is to determine if the liability outweighs the assets. In other words, is what the Customer finds objectionable about the item greater than all the things she likes about the item?

➤ A perceived drawback is nothing more than liabilities overshadowing assets.

➤ To have second thoughts about a purchase decision is normal and natural.

➤ When you fail to develop a product's assets at the beginning of the sale, you may walk away from a "right" sale.

➤ The job of a Professional Sales Associate is to make it impossible for a Customer to make a mistake.

➤ The best way to prepare yourself for objections is to practice responding to them in advance.

Chapter 7

Step Seven
The Close

You have matched your Customer's needs to the right product and exceeded her expectations by suggesting additional products, including your best solution. If you encountered an objection, you answered it. You are now ready to close.

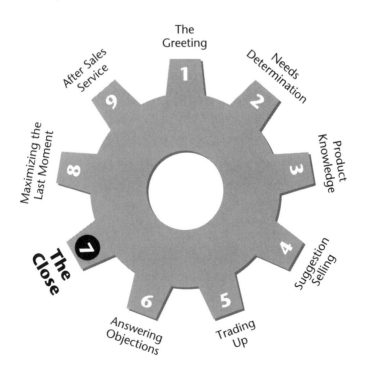

> ## The gutters and streets of countless skid rows are filled with sales people who couldn't close!
>
> *Anonymous*

The close is the natural culmination of all your efforts in the selling process. It is where "the rubber meets the road", as is often said. There are many books written about how to close a Customer, but often in the retail world you will find that if you have done your job well up to this point, the close will happen almost by itself. Rather than burden you with numerous closing strategies, some fancy and some almost dishonest, I will cover the top four closing techniques. These are the ones that you will use in 99 percent of your sales relationships. Keep in mind that if you have to revert to something really fancy or involved to close the sale, you probably shouldn't make the sale.

Buying signals

When a Customer is ready to buy, he gives off, what I call, a "Buying Signal." A Buying Signal can be verbal — the Customer will say, "I'll take it." or "It will look wonderful in my living room." or "I can't wait to show it to my friends." A Buying Signal can also be nonverbal, the Customer telling you through his actions he is ready to purchase. The most obvious example is when a Customer takes an item to the cash register by himself.

Sometimes a Buying Signal is as subtle as a man touching his back pocket to see if his wallet is there. (He has made the decision to buy and is making sure that he has the money.) Generally, non-verbal Buying Signals are very discreet and can be missed if you are not tuned in. If you suspect you have seen a non-verbal Buying Signal, simply begin to close the sale. If you fail to close the sale when a Customer gives you a Buying Signal, you may lose the sale because the Customer may talk himself out of buying the item or get confused about what he really wants.

Types of closes

1. The Either/Or Close

The most natural and easiest close of all is the "either/or" close. In this close, you assume the Customer is ready to buy because you have heard or observed a Buying Signal and, therefore, know the Customer is ready. The "either/or" is very simple and comes in a number of versions. It consists of simply asking the Customer a question like one of the following:

- "Will that be cash or charge?"
- "Do you want me to put it in a bag or would you prefer to wear it home?"
- "Do you want the green and blue or the green and red?"
- "Do you want to take it with you or should I have it delivered?"

These closes work extremely well because they are questions that require positive answers. But what do you do if the Customer says, "Wait a minute. I'm not ready to buy."?

The best response is a favorite among four year olds: Why? When a Customer has given you a Buying Signal and then balks at the close, you have to ask why. Most of us have had the question knocked out of us by age five with the (non) answer, "because." It's time to revive that old question and ask it when the Customer tells you he is not ready to buy. The answer he gives will provide you with the information necessary to close the sale. It may take the form of an objection or a request for more information. Both the hidden objection and need for more information will help you make sure that you fully understand the Customer's needs and do not sell what is not needed. The important thing is not to be put off by a failed close. It will help you make a good sale if you remember to ask why.

2. The Assume the Sale Close

In the "assume the sale" close, simply start moving the Customer to the cash wrap to ring up the sale. This very simple technique is often used when the Customer has given a very clear Buying Signal such as, "I'll take it." or "Do you take personal checks?" There is seldom ambiguity in this close. Just start walking to the register with the product, and the Customer will follow. You can add the "either/or" close if you want to sell an additional item.

3. The Balance Sheet Close

Occasionally a Customer does not give a clear Buying Signal, yet you can tell he is on the verge of saying yes. The "balance sheet" close is simply restating the benefits of the product that match expressed Customer needs. (In other words, list all the assets of the product.) If there are any negative or small details the Customer is concerned with (liabilities), mention them also. The success of this close is based on the fact that the assets outweigh the liabilities. It is used for a hesitant Customer who is closely considering all the factors. Don't attempt this close unless you have probed all the Customer's needs and matched the benefits of your product to those needs. If you have not fully developed a list of benefits, this close will not work.

4. The Last Chance Close

Caution! Only use this close if it is true. In the "last chance" close, remind the Customer of the possible lost opportunity if he does not purchase the product now. This is only to be used if there really is a chance the Customer will miss out on the product. Here are some examples of the "last chance" close:

- "This is the last one in stock, and we aren't getting any more. I would hate for you to lose the chance to own it."
- "The sale ends today, and tomorrow it goes back to regular price."
- "We may be getting more in, but we never know what colors are coming, and there may be a style change."
- "There was a Customer in earlier who wanted this and said she might be back. Since we can't put it on hold, she may come back in and buy it."

> **... remind the Customer of the possible lost opportunity if he does not purchase the product now.**

Using the "last chance" close when it is true and appropriate, is not only an excellent strategy, it is great Customer Service. If you inform the Customer of a time or quantity constraint, he will not be angry with you if he chooses to wait and misses the buying opportunity. But remember, use this close only when there is truly just one chance for the Customer.

Don't talk yourself out of a close

Many Sales Associates do not know when to stop talking. I have seen many a sale lost because the Sales Associate did not recognize a Buying Signal and move to close the sale. Sometimes there is a temptation to continue talking to your Customer, particularly if you're enjoying the exchange. Nonetheless, once you have seen or heard a

Buying Signal, your job is to close. Your Customer is telling you he is ready, willing and able to buy. If you continue to talk, you risk boring the Customer, wasting his time or confusing him. Remember the gutters and streets of countless skid rows...

How Customers behave

The close is the best part of the sale. It is your opportunity to validate all that you have done with the Customer. It is the touchdown after a long drive it is the goal after a hard play; it is the culmination of what you are and do. The close is the best time of a sale. To the Professional Sales Associate, the close is what it's all about.

Ideal distance

The ideal distance during the close is two to three feet. This is the closest you will come to the Customer. At this point the Customer trusts you, and you can, therefore, be partially within her personal space. Don't try to close a Customer while you are standing far away. The Customer expects you to be right with him at this stage.

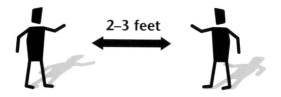

Practice

Try you own versions of the close

The Either/Or

" _____ "

" _____ "

" _____ "

The Assume the Sale

" _____ "

" _____ "

" _____ "

The Balance Sheet

" _____ "

" _____ "

" _____ "

The Last Chance

" _____ "

" _____ "

" _____ "

KEEP IN MIND:

➤ If you have to revert to something really fancy or involved to close the sale, you probably shouldn't make the sale.

➤ When a Customer is ready to buy, he gives off a "Buying Signal."

➤ Non-verbal Buying Signals are very discreet and can be missed if you are not tuned in.

➤ The most natural and easiest close of all is the "either/or" close.

➤ Closes that work extremely well take the form of questions that require positive answers.

➤ Both objections and requests for more information will help you ensure you fully understand the Customer's needs and don't sell what is not needed.

➤ Do not to be put off by a failed close.

➤ In the "assume the sale" close, simply start moving the Customer to the cash wrap to ring up the sale.

➤ The "balance sheet" close is simply restating the benefits of the product that match expressed Customer needs.

➤ The "last chance" close reminds the Customer of the possible lost opportunity if he does not purchase the product now.

➤ Don't talk yourself out of a close.

Chapter 8

Step Eight
Maximizing the Last Moment

You have shown your best solution to meet your Customer's needs. If you encountered an objection, you answered it and successfully made the sale by using the best close. Now in Step Eight you will learn how to maximize the last moment that you have with the Customer.

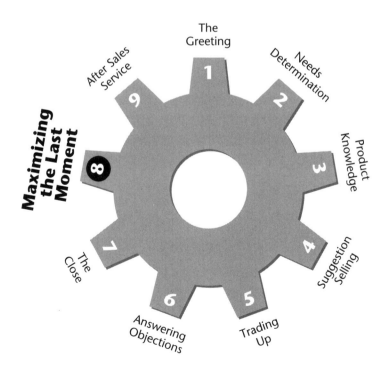

> # True eloquence consists in saying all that need be said and no more.
>
> *François, Duc de La Rochefoucauld (1613-80), French writer, moralist*

Have you ever thought about a Customer that you have not seen in some time? You might be standing in the store on a slow morning, and a face will come into your mind. You think, "I wonder what happened to Mrs. Jones? I haven't seen her for a few weeks and she used to come in almost every week." Customers sometimes do not return to a store, and there are many reasons for this. The pie chart below is a good representation of a group of surveys[8] that have been done over the years on why Customers quit shopping at a store.

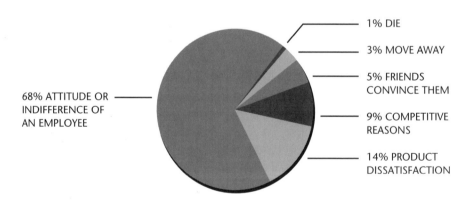

- 1% DIE
- 3% MOVE AWAY
- 5% FRIENDS CONVINCE THEM
- 9% COMPETITIVE REASONS
- 14% PRODUCT DISSATISFACTION
- 68% ATTITUDE OR INDIFFERENCE OF AN EMPLOYEE

---

[8] Compilation of Customer Satisfaction Surveys 1988–1995

Now, you can not do much to keep your Customers from moving their homes or dying, but what you can change is the 68 percent of Customers who do not return due to your indifference. That all important last impression you give the Customer, before she leaves your store, is crucial.

Every day your Customers discover something they would like to buy. As a Sales Associate, it is important to obtain a "share-of-mind" of your Customers. This means that when a need arises in your Customer, a vision of your store will immediately appear in her mind. In other words, the Customer will associate you with that product. Retailers and manufacturers spend millions of dollars in advertising to attempt to buy this share-of-mind. Yet, as a Professional Sales Associate, you can "buy" this share-of-mind for a very small price.

Share-of-mind

The key to obtaining a share-of-mind is to be aware of the importance of the last moment with the Customer, and to attempt to leave her with a lasting and positive impression of your store. Often overlooked, the last 60 seconds you spend with a Customer are crucial. Although you may be mentally moving on to the next Customer, those last 60 seconds you spend with your Customer can have a real impact on the chances of her returning to your store. In other words, the last impression will be a *lasting* impression.

Often this impression is enhanced with a simple, yet sincere, "Thank you. I really appreciate your shopping at our store." How often have you, as a Customer, thanked the clerk and heard, "You're welcome." in return? If you think about it, why did you — and not the clerk — say, "Thank you"? Could it be that the clerk thought he was doing you a favor by selling you something? This is what this usual final exchange conveys.

The power of thank you

Often the simplest things in life are the most profound. Just looking Customers in the eye while you thank them is powerful. Because Customers are so seldom honestly thanked, they often respond in an extremely positive manner. And indeed, you have good reason to thank them. After all, they took the trouble to get to your store when they could have spent their money other places or not at all. Thanking them is the least you can do.

Some other last minute memory makers

You only have about 10 seconds in which to leave that last impression. Here are some suggestions that will help Customers remember you:

- Offer your ongoing assistance. Hand them your business card. Tell them that you guarantee your products, and to call you directly if they have any questions or problems.
- If they are going to another store or place, offer them directions or help.
- Help them to their car if they have a lot of packages.
- Give them a coupon for a free drink or pastry at a nearby restaurant. (For special customers/occasions)
- Give them a small gift, such as a key chain or a magnet or anything unexpected, that shows them how much you care. (For special customers/occasions)

Examples

The following are examples of two kinds of cards that are given to Customers when they leave a store. (Front and back view.) One of these I used in Kalamazoo, Michigan, when I worked there in a department store. The other I received in a store in Newmarket, Ontario. If you were a Customer, which would you want to receive at the end of a sale? Which would give you a positive feeling about that store?

Front

Store #1

I Guarantee It!

Back

It has been a pleasure assisting you today. I hope I was able to make your visit a pleasant experience. If you are dissatisfied with your purchase in any way, please bring it to my attention. I guarantee your personal satisfaction in our merchandise and service.

Sincerely yours.

Front

Store #2

SALES POLICY

At this store we work very hard to provide you with product knowledge on the nature and value of everything we sell. We will gladly accept the return of merchandise within 30 days with proof of purchase (our cash register receipt) for Exchange or credit. Goods can be returned for reason of defect or dissatisfaction, but we exclude accidental damage and tampering. At Christmas, out of consideration to the season, we extend this facility to January 31st. At this time of year we waive proof of purchase for readily identifiable goods, but will input the lowest sales price for exchange or credit purposes.

Back

NO CASH REFUNDS

are possible, this includes credit refunds to charge cards. This is in conformity with independent industry standards and frankly is necessary if we are to remain in business. Within the boundaries of the policy, the staff is encouraged to seek your satisfaction.

Currently we charge a minimum of $7.50 for all services and repair work (silver from $12 & up) sent out of the store. Please inquire about or EXTENSIVE REPAIR SERVICES for sterling silver and fashion jewelry. Plated items do react differently with individual customers and therefore we cannot be held responsible. Please avoid applying perfume or hair spray near any jewelry. Other warranties may apply.

Practice

To really understand who your Customers are and their frame of mind, complete this sample study.

Stand out in front of your store and observe your Customers as they leave. What percentage are:

Smiling _____ %

Frowning _____ %

Bored _____ %

Ask yourself these questions:

- How many of these Customers are likely to remember that they were even in my store today?
- How many of these Customers will think of my store the next time they need a product I sell?
- How many of these Customers will tell their friends about what they just experienced? Will it be good or bad?
- How many potential Customers for life were lost today?

Here below, develop a list of additional last minute impression builders that can enhance your last minute with your Customer.

In the last 60 seconds that I spend with my Customer I can:

_____

_____

_____

_____

_____

KEEP IN MIND:

➤ You can "buy" share-of-mind for a very small price.

➤ Make the last impression a *lasting* impression.

➤ Often this impression is enhanced with a simple yet sincere, "Thank you. I really appreciate your shopping at our store."

➤ Just looking Customers in the eye while you thank them is powerful.

➤ You only have about 10 seconds in which to leave the last impression.

Chapter 9

Step Nine
After Sales Service

You have now successfully made the sale by using the best close and making that last moment with the Customer truly memorable. Now you are ready for Step Nine: building the relationship with your Customer and assuring he'll come back for more!

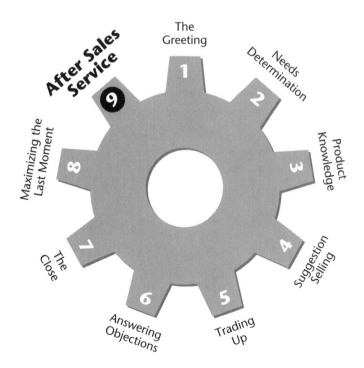

> Customers are not like buses, there isn't another coming along every twenty minutes.
>
> *Anonymous*

Customers for life

After you have completed the sale, it is time to establish a relationship with the Customer that will keep him yours for life. You have spent a great deal of effort learning about your Customer, and it would be a waste not to put that information to use in future interactions. And your Customer will appreciate it: We all like to go to places where we are known and liked.

Building Customer files

The simplest way to keep in touch with your Customers is to build a Customer file. Buy a 3" x 5" recipe box and fill it with index cards. Also pick up some alphabetized dividers. When you create a card for a Customer, start out simple. Here's an example:

Front of card:

Customer Name _____	Name of spouse _____
Address _____	Children names and dates of birth
_____	_____
City, Postal Code _____	_____
Home Phone _____	_____
Business Phone _____	_____

Phone calls at home	☐ yes ☐ no	Best Time _____	
Phone calls at work	☐ yes ☐ no	Best Time _____	
Mail at home	☐ yes ☐ no		
Mail at work	☐ yes ☐ no		

Back of card:

Item Purchased	Color	Size	Date

You can add whatever you wish to the card. The key is to start building a DataBase of your Customers. Keep track of what and when they buy. Ask them if they would like to be advised of sales in advance or if they wish to be called when something new, they might like comes in. Some Customers will not want to be called for any reason. That's fine. Ask them if you can mail them a newsletter, an advance notice of sales or just a thank-you note.

Beyond Transaction Driven Retail

Before you decide to build a DataBase of Customers, it is important to understand just how much your Customer is worth to you and your store. It is not just the $10 or $100 they spend today that matters. In fact, if a Sales Associate looks at the Customer only in terms of his purchase today, this approach is what is called "transaction driven" retail.

The key is to start building a DataBase of your Customers. Keep track of what and when they buy.

Transaction driven retail assesses the Customer only in terms of today's sale and not as a part of a life-long relationship.

Take, for example, a grocery store. Everyone shops for groceries, the average family spending about $200 a week on food. Most people have been shopping at the same grocery store for five years and will likely continue to shop at that store for another 15. The reasons people choose a certain store are obvious: location (close to home or work) and convenience.

Yet despite this long-term relationship with a grocery store, few of us can claim that our grocers know our name. Very few of us, indeed, could say that, if we stopped shopping at our local store for a month, our grocer would send us a letter inquiring about our absence.

Yet a grocery Customer is worth many thousands of dollars over a lifetime. If a Customer spends $200 a week in a grocery store, over a year his spending will total about $10,400 (52 weeks x $200). If he has shopped there for the past five years, and continues for the next 15, his spending will total $208,000 over this 20-year period.

These figures do not include the "influence factor". Have you ever gone to a store because a friend recommended it? Have you ever avoided a restaurant because a friend told you it was bad? We listen to advice from family and friends all the time, about where to get deals and where not to go. This is the influence factor: If you really like a store, you tell others to shop there too. If you happen to tell five friends, that $208,000 can become $1,248,000. On the other hand, if you really dislike a store and tell five friends, you would deprive that store of more than $1,248,000 in sales over twenty years since bad news travels much faster and more widely than good news. In short, the value of a Customer must be measured over time. Just think what could happen if a grocery store spent the time and effort in treating each Customer as if they were a million dollar sale! Just think of your Customers so impressed with your care that they become "apostles" and preach the gospel of your store!

> **One of the reasons that a Customer DataBase is so important is that it provides a method of tracking your Million Dollar Customers.**

Mining the gold in your Customer DataBase

One of the reasons that a Customer DataBase is so important is that it provides a method of tracking your Million Dollar Customers. It is a way to identify who they are, what they buy, when they buy and how they buy. If you can track this information, then you can add value to your relationship with your Customer.

Take, for instance, the Customers who like to have the newest items first. Whenever anything new comes in the store that you think they might like, pick up the phone and let them know. When a sale is coming up, phone the Customers who love a bargain. And for those Customers who need to stretch their dollars, call when you get something in that adds value to a product the Customer has purchased in the past. For example, if you know that Mr. Chow bought a pair of navy pants and a white shirt from your store last month, call him when you receive a new shipment of light blue shirts that will go well with the pants. Explain that it is a good idea to have two or three shirts to go with a pair of pants and that this adds value to his original purchase.

A Customer DataBase will help you to keep track of all the needs of all of your Customers. It helps if it is on computer, but even the simple system illustrated on page 89 will do.

Building relationships & repeat business

Here is a list of easy-to-do things to help build better relationships with your Customers and keep them coming back:

- In talking with your Customers, use their name every chance you get, especially on the phone.
- Develop an in-store DataBase or card file.
- Keep your regular Customers informed of sales, new merchandise, etc. through phone calls, post cards, newsletters, letters, faxes and E-mail. Contact a minimum of 10 Customers per day.

- Always phone Customers a few days or a week after they have made a major purchase and inquire about their satisfaction. (Never try to sell them anything else during this call!)
- Always tell Customers why they've made a good purchase. This reinforces their decision.
- Always tell your Customers that you guarantee everything you do for them.
- Always keep your promises.

Practice

Compute the value of a Customer to your store:		
Average amount spent per visit	$	
Times number of visits per year	X	
Equals total annual volume	= $	
Times 20 years of business	X	20
Equals Customer for Life value	$	
Times 10 friends/family if apostle	X	10
Equals total potential for an apostle	= $	

KEEP IN MIND:

➤ After you have completed the sale, it is time to establish a relationship with the Customer that will keep him yours for life.

➤ Build a Customer file.

➤ Ask your Customers if they would like to be advised of sales in advance or if they wish to be called when something new they might like comes in.

➤ Never call a Customer if they have told you that they do not want phone calls.

➤ Transaction driven retail assesses the Customer only in terms of today's sale and not as a part of a life-long relationship. Avoid this approach.

➤ One of the reasons a Customer Database is so important is that it provides a method of tracking your Million Dollar Customers.

➤ Phone Customers a few days or a week after they have made a major purchase and inquire about their satisfaction. (Never try to sell them anything else during this call!)

➤ Always tell your Customers that you guarantee everything you do for them.

➤ Always keep your promises.

Chapter 10

The Complaining Customer

···

You have closed the best sale you could and remembered
to make that last moment with the Customer truly memorable.
You then assured a future relationship with your Customer
so that when the Customer returns you are ready to move right
back to the greeting. Unfortunately, you may come across
a complaining or difficult Customer. This Chapter will help
you transform a difficult Customer into an apostle who
preaches the gospel of your store.

> When complaints are freely heard, deeply considered and speedily reformed, then is the utmost bound of civil liberty attained that wise men look for.
>
> *John Milton (1608-74), English poet*

In-your-face Customers

One of the more difficult issues that the Professional Sales Associate confronts is the "in-your-face" complaining Customer. Nothing is as stressful as a complaining Customer. He aggravates us, turns off other Customers in the store and generally creates havoc. Oftentimes, the complaining Customer does not even have to be in your face to make for an unpleasant experience — he can do it over the phone or from a distance. There are strategies to cope with this "in-your-face" Customer and I will explain how in the next pages.

As we discussed in the last chapter, it is difficult to have a problem with a Million Dollar Customer. If you compare a Customer who is complaining over a $50 or $250 problem to the thousands of dollars he will spend in your store over the next 10 years, you are much less likely to give him a problem over a complaint or the return of an item.

Returns

Returns are often a source of complaints from Customers. How we handle returns is both a matter of our personality and knowledge, as well as store policy. Returns come in two basic types. There is the "righteous return" and the "less than righteous return". The righteous return involves merchandise that is brought back by the Customer because either he changed his mind, and had not used (or abused) the merchandise in any way, or there is a defect in the product. The less than righteous return involves merchandise that is brought back by the Customer who has either used or abused the product or a return that does not conform to your normal policy (e.g., a Customer returns a sale item six months later when you can no longer sell it, or returns it without a receipt, and there is a question if they really purchased the item from you). Often the return that you will have the most trouble with is the "less than righteous return" because you may feel that the Customer is taking advantage of your store and is lying or trying to cheat you.

> **How you handle returns is first and foremost based on your store's policies in this area.**

How you handle returns is first and foremost based on your store's policies in this area. I can only suggest some things to consider.

The Customer loses

We generally know when something is being returned because it is going the wrong way, back in, not out of the store! When a Customer returns something to your store, how should you respond? There are a few steps that you should follow for every return, righteous or less than righteous, because in the first few minutes you generally do not know which kind of return it is.

When you see a Customer coming in the store with a return, you should approach the Customer immediately. (This is entirely different from the normal approach or greeting, which is to take a step back). As you approach the Customer, begin to immediately apologize: "I am very sorry that you had to return that item." The reason to start with an apology is that often a Customer is upset about returning something, particularly if it is damaged or defective and, if you start with an apology, it is difficult for the Customer to remain angry or upset.

The next step is to find out why the Customer is returning the item. This can be accomplished with a simple question addressing the problem with the product.

The third step is a critical step and often forgotten one. If the return is due to damage or defect, we immediately make

"How can I make it right?" Your best option is to offer an exchange to save the sale.

a statement about how unusual this is or how it never happens. This is called "validating the quality of your store". Have you ever returned a product to a store and had the clerk tell you that they have received 10 of them back in the past month? You immediately wonder why they continue to sell the junk. When you tell the Customer that this is very unusual or never happens, you are reinforcing the view of your store as a top quality store that carries only top quality merchandise, and that a damage or defect is not a common occurrence. You then apologize once more, and assure the Customer that it will never happen again.

The next step is to ask the Customer, "How can I make it right?" Your best option is to offer an exchange to save the sale. If that is not possible, a refund is required. If you give the Customer an exchange or a refund, and he leaves the store satisfied, who has lost? You could say that no one has lost because you will return the damaged or defective item to the supplier and will get your money back, and that the Customer now has what he wanted. But have you ever considered that with a return *the Customer always loses*? If a Customer needs a product, and she comes to your store to buy it and has to make a second trip to return it, then that second trip takes time for the Customer. If you believe that the Customer's time is worth something (her hourly pay, for example) then you realize that the twenty minutes or two hours that he has spent to come back to your store a second time is waste of his time. The Customer loses time whenever he has to return an item to a store. The Professional Sales Associate knows this, and therefore adds a final step to the return process.

The final step in the return process is to give the Customer a "perk" for his time and trouble. It is a way of compensating the Customer and saying, "I'm sorry." in a more concrete way. The perk can be a small gift certificate or an additional item or an upgrade to a better product. You offer the perk, not as full compensation for the trouble that the Customer experienced, but as partial compensation. ("I'm very sorry that you had to make a trip to return this today. I'd like you to have this $5 gift certificate as a small token of apology. I realize how valuable your time is, and I can never fully compensate you for your trouble, but I would like to do something to say how sorry I am.")[9]

The less than righteous return

How do you handle the Customer who returns something that is not damaged or defective, or is one year old, or has been misused? First, ask yourself what percentage of people have a conscience — can tell the difference between right and wrong?

If you said 99 percent you are right. (The other one percent are sociopaths and have no conscience). If a person has a conscience, however, does it mean that he never lies or breaks rules? Of course not. All of us do things that we are not proud of after we do them. The Customer who returns an item and lies to us about it will feel guilt. The amount of

---

[9]   This must follow your store policy. Do not give anything to a Customer that you have not been authorized to give.

the guilt will depend on the individual and how much he shades the truth. But most people will feel guilty about lying to a store, especially if the store treats them as if they were telling the truth. The Customer who is treated as if he were not lying when he is, will try to get rid of the guilt by buying more in the store and telling his friends how great the store is.

Can you ever be sure the Customer is lying? I have seen many cases of a Customer falsely accused of lying. There is no greater mistake you can make than falsely accusing an innocent person. Ask yourself: can you prove in a court of law that the Customer is lying? Do you have a video of him wearing the product last night, of putting it in a dishwasher, of dropping it on the floor, or any other act that you suspect? The answer is obviously no. There is always the possibility the Customer is telling the truth. You have to treat the less than righteous return the same as the righteous return. The investment you make in the loss caused by that return can, in most cases, be made up in increased purchases by that Customer. Would you lose thousands of dollars in future business because of a $50 return?

Three strikes and you're out!

Can you afford to sell to sociopaths? How about the Customers who regularly "rent" products? They constantly try to return products they have used or abused and take advantage of your policy. I recommend the "three strikes and you're out" rule.[10] Rather than taking the risk of falsely accusing an innocent Customer, handle the less than righteous return the same as the righteous return, but *keep track of the less than righteous*. When you have to exchange or refund a product that you suspect, enter that Customer's

---

[10] Again, this must be a policy of your store.

name, address and phone number in a list. Strike One.
If in the next year you have a second less than righteous
return from that same Customer, again handle it as a righteous return, but track it. Strike Two. If in the next twelve
months, the Customer again returns an item
you feel is wrong, inform the Customer
you're sorry, but it appears you are not able
to meet his expectations. Explain that over
the past year he has brought back three
items you felt were not justified. Remind
him you accommodated him on the first
two returns, but are sorry that you can no
longer do it. Tell him you feel badly that he
cannot be satisfied by your products, and
you would like him to have this $5 gift certificate for the
store down the street. (Send them to the competition:
This is war!).

> **You cannot afford to have sociopaths as Customers, but more importantly, you cannot afford to treat your good Customers as sociopaths.**

With the "three strike" policy, you will never falsely accuse
an innocent Customer (and create a 'Terrorist' who could
actively try to destroy your business), and you will not lose
thousands of dollars of potential business by turning off a
Customer who "fell off the straight and narrow" one time.
You cannot afford to have sociopaths as Customers, but
more importantly, you cannot afford to treat your good
Customers as sociopaths.

Nice Customers will put you out of business!

It is the nice Customer who will put a store out of business.
The nice Customer is the one who hates to make a scene,
never complains and never comes back with a return. It's
the nice Customer, for instance, who after eating a bad
meal in a restaurant, will tell the waiter if he asks, it was
fine. As the nice Customer leaves, he's saying to himself,

"I'm never coming back here again." And if the food was really bad, he'll tell his friends and family to steer clear of the place. When the nice Customer goes away, he sometimes takes many potential Customers with him.

The real secret service

As owners of the restaurant in the above example, most of us, not only would want to know what the Customer thinks, we would want to ensure the dinner was replaced immediately and the Customer was more than satisfied. The real secret of complaining Customers is not only to make it right, but to add a perk as a way of saying sorry for the disappointment. In the case of the restaurant, the dinner would be replaced and then, as a perk, the Customer would receive a free desert or not be charged for the dinner. When this is done, you not only save the situation, you transform a potential terrorist into an apostle: The Customer will now preach how wonderful your business is, rather than destroying your business by relaying its weaknesses.

Helping Customers to vent

Most complaining Customers are just like you and me. They are normal people who expect to get what they pay for. They are also normal in that they occasionally lose their temper. Although losing one's temper is a safety mechanism that keeps us sane, when Customers lose their temper, it can be hard not to take it personally. Yet if you remind yourself a Customer's anger is not directed at you personally, then the temper tantrum loses its power to frighten or anger you in return.

The worst thing you can do when a Customer yells is to yell back. This is like throwing gasoline onto a fire. You need to take a small step back and allow the Customer to vent. Just like a tea kettle that has too much steam in it, the hot air needs out. If you let the Customer vent rather than confront him, then once the steam blows off, the Customer will feel very foolish. This is called the "reflective method" of dealing with confrontation. Instead of taking it personally, you give the Customer space to get it out. Thankfully, Customers do not yell often, but be prepared when they do. In the very rare case of a really abusive Customer, it is acceptable to ask the Customer to leave the store, in as nice of a manner as possible. Although we always remain pleasant, there is that very rare Customer (really one in thousands for most stores) who does not deserve our attention.

Turning a Complaining Customer into an Apostle

The secret to success in retailing is the ability to turn complaining Customers into Customers who are so much in love with your store that they preach its attributes to everyone they meet. Transforming a complaining Customer into an apostle who preaches the gospel of your store, however, takes real skill.

> **The secret to success in retailing is the ability to turn complaining Customers into Customers who are so much in love with your store that they preach its attributes to everyone they meet.**

One of the best ways to affect this turnaround is to understand that the Customer sees the situation from a very different perspective than you may. His perspective is often made up of very different factors than you might imagine. He does not see the store or products in the same way that you do. The Customer, for instance, has made the effort to come to your store and to do business with you. Sometimes that effort is considerable. It may involve driving a car and parking, or walking to your store. In some cases, it may even involve scheduling baby-sitting, foregoing another activity or just creating time to shop. The Customer has chosen you to give his money to. This effort alone makes the Customer special. When he complains, therefore, it is often a sign that something he expected did not happen.

Here is a list of some of the things Customers expect:

- A quality product without defects.
- Professional Sales Associates who can answer their questions.
- Professional Sales Associates who know everything about a product.
- Products in stock.
- Competitive prices.
- An advertised item on hand and clearly visible.
- A courteous and cheerful refund if the product is not right.

If you listen to your complaining Customer, you will hear what he expects. When you know what he expects and yet fail to deliver, have an apology and a perk ready. The apology is necessary to tell the Customer that you are truly sorry for disappointing him: The perk is the icing on the cake, the act that turns the complaining Customer into your store's apostle.

Perks

What exactly is a perk? It is anything unexpected that you can give a disappointed Customer. It is a special gift that goes beyond saying, "I'm sorry." Some examples of perks are:

- A $5 gift certificate.
- A $25 gift certificate.
- A gift certificate for a coffee and muffin.
- A gift certificate for gasoline.
- A certificate for free alterations on their next purchase.
- A certificate for a dinner for two at a nice restaurant.

The size and value of the perk should be somehow equal to the wrong the Customer feels he has suffered. Do not give a $50 dinner to a Customer who was upset about not finding a five dollar advertised item. Instead, offer to replace the five dollar item with a six or seven dollar item at the advertised price.

A perk should not be casually thrown around. It is a valuable method of building and maintaining Customer goodwill, but it will not do this if it is put into a formula or made standard for each situation. To be effective, perks must be "custom made" at the time at which they are needed. This is the job of the Professional Sales Associate and only the Professional Sales Associate. Store managers cannot do it, buyers cannot do it; only the person standing in front of the Customer can make the decision as to what the perk should be. Identify things that your store is prepared to give as perks, and have them ready for when you need them. All it takes are a few Customers that you treat "above and beyond the call," and word will spread about how terrific your store is. Know thy perks and use them — they'll keep Customers coming back!

Practice

What "Perks" are available at your store? List them and
the situation in which you might use them.

Perk	I would use it when...

KEEP IN MIND:

➤ How you handle returns is both a matter of your personality and knowledge, as well as store policy.

➤ How you handle returns is first and foremost based on your store's policies and practices. Never do anything that violates these policies.

➤ Returns come in two basic types. There is the "righteous return" and the "less than righteous return".

➤ When you see a Customer coming in the store with a return, you should approach the Customer immediately with an apology for his trouble.

➤ Determine what the problem is, then apologize.

➤ Validate the quality of your store, then apologize

➤ Make it right by offering an exchange, not a refund.

➤ Add a perk as a way of saying sorry for the disappointment.

➤ With a return the Customer always loses.

➤ Keep track of the "less than righteous returns".

➤ You cannot afford to have sociopaths as Customers, but more importantly, you cannot afford to treat your good Customers as sociopaths and run the risk of creating a "terrorist".

➤ Don't take a Customer's temper tantrum personally.

➤ Develop strategies to turn a complaining Customer into a Customer who is so much in love with your store that he preaches its attributes to everyone he meets.

Chapter 11

Building Your Career as a Professional Sales Associate

> I would rather be the man who bought the Brooklyn Bridge than the one who sold it.
>
> *Will Rodgers*

Where do I go from here?

Now that you have reached the end of this book, along with the suggested exercises, you will no doubt be anxious to continue building your career as a Professional Sales Associate. Although many stores are now realizing the importance of hiring and keeping Professional Sales Associates, one of the realities you will encounter is that of selling-cost ratios. All retail stores, and indeed all businesses that sell a product, look at the cost of selling that product. If the cost of selling a product is too high, either the price of the product increases or the company loses money and goes out of business. The harsh reality of business is that every component of a business must "pay its way". Normally in a specialty retail store the cost of selling (payroll dollars divided by total sales dollars) can be as high as 15 percent, but averages about 10 percent. Supermarkets and high volume "vending machine" retailers will average as low as two percent of sales to payroll. For the average retailer, 10 percent is the right amount to spend on payroll. (55 percent goes to purchase the products, 12 percent to pay the rent, and 15 percent for expenses such as supplies, phone, utilities, buying trips, depreciation [replacing fixtures and carpeting and lighting every five years or so] and other back office expenses.) This leaves about eight percent for net profit.

Net profit is the return that the shareholders expect for their investment in the store, and it is also necessary to purchase new equipment and fixtures. Net profit is necessary to keep people investing and employed in retail businesses.

How much do I have to sell?

If 10 percent is the average percentage for selling salaries, then in order to make $30,000 a year, you must sell $300,000 worth of product ($30,000 is 10% of $300,000). To determine the salary you expect to make, divide your total product sales by 10. Clearly there are some stores that will have a very hard time paying even one person $15,000 a year, much less two people $40,000. Look, therefore, at the total volume that you can realistically sell in a store. Do the above math to see if you can really make the income you desire. You really contribute to the success of a store when you sell to your potential, and it would be a crazy store that did not reward you for that. You must prove your worth, then the money will follow.

Where can I learn more?

This book certainly does not contain all there is to know about selling, although it comes close! For further reading on selling and retailing, I have included a short bibliography at the end of the book. But don't forget, that your fellow Professional Sales Associates can be a great source of information and learning. The next time you go for coffee or a break, rather than talking about the movie you saw last week, try to exchange ideas about how to better work with a difficult objection, or share a new Needs Determination question that worked well. You might also compare successful closing techniques. Every Customer you work with is an education. The old cliché that "good retailers are students of their Customers" holds much truth. You can get a great education if you just listen and learn.

The lessons that you learn as a Professional Sales Associate will help you in all parts of your life and career. I know you can effect many lives for the better when you know how to satisfy Customer's needs, and this is why I have dedicated my time and energy to helping others become Professional Retail Sales Associates. Becoming a Professional Retail Sales Associate is not an easy task, and sometimes you will be discouraged. You must always remember what brought you to this profession, your love and respect of people. That love and respect will carry you through the tough times. I have given you the tools, now you have to take them, use them and build your Professional Career. I hope that you will measure everything you learned in this book against the reality of your store and experience. Take the best of each and perfect your skills.

Good Luck.

J.E.D

Appendix

Answers to Chapter 2 Quiz

1. Customers usually know what they want.

FALSE. Customers usually only have *an idea* of what they want. If they knew exactly what they wanted, then they could get it from a vending machine or order it from a catalog. Most Customers rely on the Professional Sales Associate to help them find what will really meet their needs. Research[11] tells us that almost 80 percent of purchase decisions are made *after* a Customer enters a store. Customers change their mind because their mind, in most cases, was not made up.

2. Most Customers want to be left alone when shopping.

FALSE. Customers certainly don't want a vulture on their shoulder or a school of piranha circling them, but they do want answers to questions and informed assistance. The reason Customers come to a specialty store is for the service and selection. This said, maintaining the proper distance from the Customer in each step of the sale is critical.

3. Many people buy when they are unhappy.

TRUE. Shopping is the world's best and most expensive anti-depressant. This is despite the fact that it would undoubtedly be cheaper to get an anti-depressant drug from a doctor than to go shopping! Still, many people use the process of shopping to buy things that symbolize what they can't obtain in their lives.

---

[11] Ad Council 1994

4. Customers cannot be persuaded to buy something they say they don't want.

FALSE. People often say things they really don't mean. Have you ever said, "I hate you!" or "I'll never buy in that store again." It is very common for people in the heat of a moment to say something in anger or fright that they regret or retract moments later. When your Customer says, "I think it is too expensive." or "It's the wrong color.", you need to remember people often change their minds with more information. How many times have Customers claimed a product was wrong or too expensive only to change their mind minutes later when they discover that, by comparison to other products, the product is not so wrong or too expensive. Customers need the time and space to change their minds gracefully. You need to listen between the lines and not force them to make a decision. If you don't make a big deal of their rejection early on, they will feel better about accepting re-introduction of a certain product later in the sale.

5. In times of tight money, Customers buy only what they need.

FALSE. If Customers only bought what they need, our economy would probably fall apart! Most purchases are not absolutely necessary for our survival, but do help our sense of well-being. Customers can and will buy when the purchase is felt to be an Investment (big I) and not to be a capricious act. Even in tight times, Customers will allow themselves small luxuries to boost their spirits.

6. What Customers ask for is not always what they want.

TRUE. It is very common that Customers' *stated* needs are sometimes not their *real* needs. In some cases, Customers themselves are not really sure of their underlying need. They are always sure, however, after the sale, of whether the item they purchased met the need or not.

7. Most Customers have a price limit on their shopping needs.

FALSE. What most Customers have is a *price expectation* — what they expected to pay for the item. This is true, especially for less frequent purchases. We may remember that the last time we bought jeans they were around $40. However, if this time we also want a designer name on our jeans, this will affect the price. Often Customers have an expectation of price that is based on incorrect assumptions, such as what they paid for the item 10 years ago or for a similar but lower quality item they saw in a store window. Your job is to help Customers to understand the price. When Customers say, "That's too expensive.", what they are in effect saying is, "You have not really explained why this item costs this much." A price complaint is really a misunderstanding about the value of an item.

8. Yesterday's luxuries are today's necessities.

TRUE. Most of what you sell today is really not necessary. We live in a society that is built around making its members feel better. Many of the products you sell are in reality luxuries. They are not necessary for survival. But they are important to people. Imagine if every car just had a vinyl bench seat and plain brown dashboard, or if all clothing was made from the same material and of the same color. Products add newness to our lives and bring joy to Customers. A luxury is not a bad thing: It makes our lives more enjoyable.

9. Shopping can be an emotionally rewarding experience.

TRUE. This is just barely true today. A few years ago, research showed that most people enjoyed shopping and found it rewarding. Today, research tells us Customers no longer find shopping to be fun or enjoyable. In fact, many shoppers report that shopping is "a drudgery, no fun, a job, a hassle, lots of problems."[12] Think of the future of your job if all your Customers preferred to shop from a computer, a phone or a television. It is up to you to make shopping more enjoyable — nothing less than your career depends on it!

10. Spending money makes people happy.

TRUE. Buying is a joyful experience. It makes people happy to acquire the things they desire. But they are even happier if what they buy lasts, and if it is right for them. Once again, this is where you come in.

---

[12] Wall Street Journal, Survey of Shopping Habits in North America, 1994.

Additional Reading

Dion, James and Topping, Ted. *Start and Run a Profitable Retail Business.*
Bellingham, WA: Self-Counsel Press, 2002.
Johnson, Spenser. *The One Minute Sales Person.*
New York, NY: Avon Books, 1984.

Girard, Joe. *How to Sell Anything to Anybody.*
New York: Bantam Books, 1977.

Girard, Joe. *How to Close Every Sale.*
New York: Warner Books, 1989.

Hopkins, Tom. *How to Master the Art of Selling.*
Scotsdale, AZ: Champion Press.

Willingham, Ron. *The Best Seller.*
New Jersey: Prentice-Hall, 1984.

Will, Gregory L. *And it Tastes Just Like Chicken.*
Burr Ridge, IL: Irwin Publishing, 1994.

Index

About Dionco Inc.

Jim Dion is an experienced, proven professional with a deep knowledge of his subjects. His thoroughly researched and individually tailored presentations focus on key issues affecting all organizations. A gifted communicator, it is ultimately his obvious concern for people and his commitment to increasing the individual and organizational success of his clients, that make Jim one of the most effective and sought after speakers internationally and in North America. Jim designs a wide range of keynote addresses to communicate and cascade strategic transformation and tactical change messages into organizations. Additionally, Jim develops a series of customized interactive workshops that provide highly practical and important skills for successful transformation efforts.

Jim's philosophy is that speeches and workshops have to accomplish three goals. They must be:
- **Enlightening**. The information provided must be something that is new or different
- **Practical**. The information provided has to work back in the real world and not just be theory
- **Entertaining**. People learn more when they are enjoying themselves

Skills training and future trends reviews all aim at the same result: helping people balance the reality or the requirements of today against the unknown of tomorrow. It's all about change: defining, explaining, understanding and finally doing it! Jim has been delivering keynote speeches, seminars, and training workshops for over 20 years.

Dionco Inc.
300 West Grand Avenue, Suite 408
Chicago, IL 60610
312 673-0187
http://www.dionco.com
jimdion@dionco.com

Dionco Inc.
350 W. Hubbard St. Suite 240
Chicago, IL 60610
312 835-5552

About the Author

Jim Dion is founder and president of Dionco Inc., Chicago. Jim is an internationally known consultant, keynote speaker, trainer, author and one of North America's leading experts on retail technology, retail selling & service, merchandising & operations as well as consumer trends that impact retail.

Jim started his retail career in 1964 in a men's wear store in Chicago. He was appointed Store Manager in 1971. From 1972 to 1974 he was night Manager of the Sheraton Chicago Hotel in downtown Chicago. From 1975 to 1981 he was employed by Sears Canada where he started in Retail Management in Richmond Hill, Ontario and moved to the Toronto Catalog Center in an operating position. He was promoted to Buyer, Jeanswear and was responsible for buying and marketing for 68 retail and 958 catalog stores. In 1981 he left Sears to become National Sales Training Manager for Levi Strauss. During his time with Levi Strauss he developed one of the most advanced Sales Training Programs in the industry, in addition to introducing a Just-in-Time inventory system to Levi Strauss factories. From 1985 to 1988 he was Executive Vice President of Gilmore's Department stores in Kalamazoo, Michigan where he repositioned a 106-year-old chain in a highly competitive retail environment.

Jim has taught at Laurier University, Ryerson University and the International Academy of Fashion Merchandising and Design in Chicago. Jim is a frequent speaker for the National Retail Federation in Washington DC on Technology, Inventory Control, Negotiation Techniques and Store Management. In addition, he has co-authored the "Start and Run a Retail Business" for Self-Council Press.

Jim consults with numerous Retailers in the U.S. and internationally. He is a recognized expert in the North American PC market and a Microsoft Developer. Jim also studies and evaluates new retail POS, EDI, merchandising systems and relationship marketing software. He was a judge for the Microsoft® Retail Developer Awards as well as a Judge for CIO Magazine Top 100. Jim has presented over 150 technology workshops across the country for the National Retail Federation, Microsoft, IBM and Nortel. As well, Jim lectures and writes for numerous trade and national magazines on technology issues and on the Internet and its use and misuse by retailers and manufacturers and has been featured on Fox News and NBC. He is also a faculty member of Harley-Davidson University in Milwaukee, WI.

He graduated from Chicago State University in Chicago, Illinois BS, MS Ed in 1971 and Illinois Institute of Technology Ph.D. (abd) in Industrial Psychology and Marketing in 1975.